"Following her initial book on human embodiment, *Struggling with Body Image: Seeing What God Sees*, Lainey Greer offers a significant expansion of this critical issue with *Embodied Holiness*. If readers wonder why this topic is important, Greer offers a simple answer: 'God expects in his followers a physical well-being sufficient to simply carry out what he commands.' The first word in her response—God—underscores Greer's foundational approach in her book: The triune God is intimately involved with his embodied image bearers, whom he redeems and calls to a life of embodied holiness. With this work, Greer makes a much-needed contribution to a theology of the body."

—**Gregg R. Allison**, professor of Christian theology, The Southern Baptist Theological Seminary, and secretary, Evangelical Theological Society

"Dr. Lainey Greer's *Embodied Holiness* offers a compelling and well-researched exploration of the Christian responsibility to honor God through the body. Greer perceptively highlights the persistent tendency in the church to elevate the soul while devaluing the body, a mindset rooted in gnostic influences. She counters this tendency with a biblically grounded understanding of the body's worth. With practical guidance and heartfelt reflections, Greer challenges readers to pursue embodied holiness, embracing the body as a vessel for God's glory. Her work is a timely call to address misconceptions about the body and live out an integrated faith that reflects God's design in a fragmented world."

—**David Closson**, director, Center for Biblical Worldview, Family Research Council

"Holiness is an often overlooked or misunderstood concept among many Christians, and even more overlooked is holiness in relation to our bodies. In *Embodied Holiness*, Greer surveys biblical, anthropological, theological, and historical foundations to urge us toward a faithful valuing and stewarding of our physical bodies. Helpfully, she concludes with specific assessments and applications that direct her readers from understanding to action. Her work is a much-needed call for we image bearers who routinely ignore and abuse our bodies."

—**Ryan C. Hanley**, chair of missions and ministry and associate professor of biblical studies, University of the Cumberlands

"Lainey Greer's *Embodied Holiness* is a timely and necessary correction to the all-too-common disregard for the body's role in a flourishing life dedicated to God. Greer grounds the body's value and its centrality in our lives as Christians with theological precision. She then applies these insights with practical wisdom and sensitivity to provide a valuable resource that will serve the church for years to come."

—**Joseph Hussung**, senior counselor, Fieldstone Counseling

"Our bodies greatly matter, yet far too often the church has neglected the value and place of our physicality. Thankfully, Lainey Greer joins others who are helping us think more carefully about this topic. Part of what makes Dr. Greer's work so valuable is that she writes both from personal experience and in light of her scholarly research. I am grateful her voice has been added to this important conversation."

—**Kelly M. Kapic**, professor of theological studies, Covenant College

"When God created humans in his image and likeness, he created them embodied. The gospel promises the resurrection of the dead—the glorification of the human person, including the body. Greer surveys the biblical teaching on the body and shows how pervasive is the goodness of embodied existence for humans in the Scriptures. Her book includes several chapters of implications and applications; the result is an excellent holistic biblical and theological treatment of embodiment."

—**Glenn R. Kreider**, editor in chief, *Bibliotheca Sacra*, and professor of theological studies, Dallas Theological Seminary

"The ancient serpent wants to keep this quiet. Long have we fed on half-truths about our bodies. Now we face the maladies of modern life, and so few seem to realize it. Some awaken, and soon the pendulum swings. Among the competing visions, Lainey Greer sounds a clear and balanced call.

She grounds her work in the riches of Christian Scripture and theology. Biblical voices—and especially that apostle of the body, Paul—give her bearings to both glean from the great tradition and challenge it. This leads to a realistic 'way forward' on the brass tacks of diet, sleep, and exercise. Many Christians will be pressed to think in fresh ways about their own bodies—that is, in very old ways. I pray many pastors will be among them."

—**David Mathis**, senior teacher and executive editor, Desiring God, and pastor, Cities Church, Saint Paul, Minnesota

"The mind-body interaction has been overlooked for far too long in biblical counseling. Dr. Greer brings theological clarity to the psychosomatic interaction that points to God's design for human flourishing. To grow in godliness, we must recognize that 'the believer's body is a temple of the Spirit, not a tomb for the soul.' This book should be on the shelves of all pastors, counselors, and ministry leaders."

—**Angela Shelton**, founder and executive director, Connection Point Biblical Counseling

Embodied Holiness

THE
BIBLICAL
CALL TO
BODILY
CARE

Embodied Holiness

LAINEY GREER

B&H
ACADEMIC®
BRENTWOOD, TENNESSEE

Embodied Holiness: The Biblical Call to Bodily Care

Published by B&H Academic®
Brentwood, Tennessee

ISBN: 978-1-4300-9394-7

Dewey Decimal Classification: 128
Subject Heading: BODY IMAGE \ HUMAN BODY \ GNOSTICISM

Cover design by Lindy Kasler. Cover images from Shutterstock and Stocksy. Illustration of person by Lindy Kasler.

Printed in the United States of America

30 29 28 27 26 25 VP 1 2 3 4 5 6 7 8 9 10

CONTENTS

ABBREVIATIONS

ANF	*The Ante-Nicene Fathers*. Edited by Alexander Roberts and James Donaldson. 1885–1887. 10 vols. Repr., Hendrickson, 1994.
LXX	Septuagint
NPNF[1]	*The Nicene and Post-Nicene Fathers*, Series 1. Edited by Philip Schaff. 1886–1889. 14 vols. Repr., Peabody, MA: Hendrickson, 1994.

Introduction

Understanding Embodiment

After completing my doctoral work, which focused on a biblical understanding of the body, a professor of biblical counseling at a major evangelical seminary approached me with an odd request: If you ever publish, please do not include anywhere that the body is part of the image of God.[1] I was stunned by this appeal, given

[1] While some Christians have ardently defended the body's value and importance in the Christian life, the professor's mindset toward the body is nothing new among believers. John Kilner explains:

> Many understate it by suggesting that the body is really not part of being in God's image at all. Several commentators see this as the view instinctively held by most Christians. Others find that many, even most,

that creation, the incarnation, and resurrection are such consequential Christian beliefs involving the body, and I realized the church held a worse misunderstanding of the body's value than I had thought. Now, thinking back on a variety of life events leading up to that moment, I see how the Lord pieced together my unique path toward discerning a biblical view of the body, one that culminates in an embodied—meaning tangible or in physical form—understanding of holiness.

After earning a bachelor's degree in exercise science from the University of Tennessee, personal training and nutrition certifications, and a master's degree in Christian leadership from Dallas Theological Seminary, and after subsequently

---

> theologians affirm this view. Exclusion of the body from God's image is prominent in the Alexandrian school of the early church (Clement, Origen, Athanasius, Basil, Gregory Nazianzen, Gregory of Nyssa, Cyril, etc.). The writings of commentators such as Augustine and Calvin also appear to reflect it.

John F. Kilner, *Dignity and Destiny: Humanity in the Image of God* (Eerdmans, 2015), 306. Kilner's book exists because such low views of the body persist in the church today. Thankfully, standing on the shoulders of the apostle Paul, Irenaeus, Tertullian, and others, contemporary Christians can discern a biblical view of the body that calls for bodily care.

working ten years in church ministry, I pursued a PhD in systematic theology from the Southern Baptist Theological Seminary, where I focused on human embodiment. Years before, I had worked as a personal trainer and in church ministry, where I experienced stress-related health issues, saw coworkers battle similar physical effects while in ministry, recognized the overlap between Christianity and the obesity epidemic, and witnessed the health of fellow seminary students decline one semester after the next.[2] My education and experiences, combined with an in-depth biblical and theological study of the body, led me to question, As much as it lies within our control, is God honored if his children are spiritually healthy but physically unwell? Furthermore, as Christians, how can we treat our bodies in ways that honor the Lord while managing the responsibilities of life and ministry? Surely, in God's original design and

[2] Erin F. Johnston et al., "Seminary Students and Physical Health: Beliefs, Behaviors, and Barriers," *Journal of Religion and Health* 61, no. 2 (2022): 1207–25, http://doi.org/10.1007/s10943-021-01480-7. The findings from this study revealed the clear need to address the disparity between seminary students' behaviors and the betterment of their health. Setting good health habits before entering ministry is critical for long-term ministry service.

before the fall, day-to-day living and lifestyle choices were not a strain on the body. The body was to be reckoned a creational gift and one to steward, not to overlook and neglect in ways that threaten our health and ministry effectiveness. But in many ways, this is the troublesome predicament we as Christians find ourselves in.

Christianity and the Body

My doctoral work solidified the realization that the issue was far deeper than Christians failing to care for their physical health. The real issue is our very conception of the body, a conception that I first had to personally correct before I could encourage others to do the same. Some years before beginning my PhD, I was anorexic and over-exercised. I turned to these body-abusing behaviors to deal with a difficult trial, and despite being a believer, I willfully chose to damage my body. After a couple of years of these behaviors and their resulting health consequences, I sensed the Holy Spirit's conviction. I was harming his temple, his dwelling place. I had been bought at a price. I was not my own. Still, I was far from glorifying God in my body (1 Cor 6:19–20). Combine that realization with adverse health effects of ministry stress, my doctoral study, and years of discerning what it meant to care for my body without obsession or excess, and the result is a book on embodied holiness. And while I still struggle in various ways to honor God in my body, that firm desire to do so is there, as I know it is through my body that I display my devotion to him. From this context, I hope to convince you of the call to embodied holiness.

As I once did, most people probably go through their day without considering how mundane decisions such as eating, drinking, sitting, exercising, or sleeping impact their body and overall well-being. While Christians must not prioritize these physical matters over spiritual ones, we are still compelled to care for our health. As we will see, a biblical understanding of the body presents the responsibility of bodily care while we await our eternal condition of perfected well-being. These arguments are to come, but for now, we must be informed on some introductory themes.

Christianity and physicality coincide in kneeling in prayer, worshipping God, reading Scripture, comforting the hurting, practicing hospitality, feeding the poor, singing, caring for the sick, utilizing spiritual gifts, spreading the gospel, and more. It is through physicality that the glorious God condescended to inglorious humanity, revealing himself through the beauty of his creation, through the

Spirit-inspired Word, and ultimately through his embodied Son. John testified to touching the Son's tangible, resurrected body (1 John 1:1) so that others would have confidence in the risen Christ. It is with our ears and eyes that we hear and read the Word; it is through our divinely designed physical senses that God accommodates himself to humanity (Eph 1:13; Rev 1:3). Through the beauty of nature, God made his invisible qualities plain since the creation of the world so that his embodied image-bearers might respond in awe, coming to know him in the precise time and place he determined them to live (Rom 1:19–20; Acts 17:24–28). Even more, Christians believe in a God who both creates and resurrects bodies, who became embodied in the incarnation of God the Son to bodily atone for sin, and who indwells our bodies by his Spirit to empower us for holy living. Since we are commanded to glorify God in our bodies (1 Cor 6:20), physicality is an important part of our faith. Because "Christianity finds expression through the body, it is an embodied faith."[3]

---

[3] Lainey Greer, "The Utilization of a Theology of Human Embodiment to Address Body Image" (PhD diss., The Southern Baptist Theological Seminary, 2021), 42, https://repository.sbts.edu/bitstream/handle/10392/6643/Greersbts_0207D10687.pdf?sequence=1&isAllowed=y.

Scripture seems to assume a modicum of fitness. As far as it lies within our control, the expectation of basic physical health seems an obvious reality, but one that needs clarifying in our day and age. From God's placement of Adam in Eden to tend the garden (Gen 2:15), to David's prolific skills as a shepherd and warrior (1 Samuel 17–19), to the disciples' capacity to travel great distances on foot (Acts 1:8), God expects in his followers a physical well-being sufficient to simply carry out what he commands. Can one tend a garden, go to war, or traverse vast distances and terrains to evangelize the lost if limited by self-inflicted poor physical health? To "go" with the gospel communicates the underlying assumption that one can physically go (Matt 28:18–20). Certainly, there are physical limitations and bodily conditions that arise from birth, accidents, or other complicating health factors, which can be out of our control. These realities do not need to restrict one's ability to evangelize. After all, God often uses the fragility of our humanity to magnify himself. Consider Moses's stutter (Exod 4:10–11), the man born blind (John 9:2–3), or Paul's thorn in the flesh (2 Cor 12:7–10). I am instead speaking of willful lifestyle choices, such as those that produce excess weight and often lead to chronic disease, as these outcomes can limit our capacity to go with the gospel. Similarly, as I know quite well, one can also hamper one's physical health and ministry ability through willful starvation, overexercise, and other behaviors associated with eating disorders.

Notwithstanding illnesses, disabilities, and disorders that naturally result from the fallen world, a vibrant, faithful Christian life reckons physical health necessary to live out God's calling and to honor him as responsible, embodied image-bearers who steward his magnificent creation of the physical body.

Still, acceptance of these truths and the assumption of a healthy body seem at times, disconnected from our contemporary Christian experience. This reality is evident in a variety of forms: the overlap between the obesity epidemic and Christianity; the burnout experienced by ministry leaders; eating disorders or self-harming behaviors among believers; the prevalence of body-enhancing plastic surgeries or steroids and supplements to generate fake or exaggerated musculature; the obsession with exercise, from CrossFit, marathon running, and bodybuilding to following all things fitness on social media; and even our propensity for quick weight-loss methods rather than addressing lifestyle factors. Christians face the danger of limiting our ability to honor God through our physical bodies, which is precisely why we must allow Scripture to confront and guide our treatment of our physical well-being. Therefore, in this book, I will argue that as God's image-bearers, devoted Christians must recognize the body's value and associate it with the biblical call to bodily care. This is the way of embodied holiness.

Critical Concepts

This book is far more than a superficial contemplation of Christian fitness, as the correction of deeply rooted theological misapprehensions drives my argument. Thus, a few more preliminary tracks must be laid down, as the way believers think about the body informs their stewardship of it, or lack thereof. Because Christians ought not to think so little of the vessel that fuels our capacity for holy living, the construction of my argument first relies on an understanding of holiness as devotion or consecration to God.[4] After all, believers submit and dedicate their whole selves to God, a bodily sacrifice offered as an act of spiritual worship that God reckons holy and acceptable (Rom 12:1).

---

[4] Peter J. Gentry, "The Meaning of 'Holy' in the Old Testament," *Bibliotheca Sacra* 170, no. 680 (October 2013), 413.

Before going further, we need to understand the four areas linked with a Christian conception of the body, as this book covers three of them. While I treat the topic of body image elsewhere, it is the fourth aspect of a well-rounded biblical understanding of the body.[5]

The terminology relevant to the Christian's call to bodily care is a theology of the body, embodiment, and body stewardship. The first, foundational layer is a theology of the body, which examines Scripture's address of corporeal existence and answers the question, What basic beliefs about the body should Christians affirm? Categorizing and clarifying important beliefs about the body is especially critical in our current culture, which is simultaneously anti-body and body obsessed. As interest in a theology of the body has grown in recent years, there have been a variety of approaches to defining how Christians should understand the body.

Pope John Paul II should be credited as the first leader to present a comprehensive treatment of the theology of the body. His lengthy and groundbreaking endeavor, encompassing far more than the topics in this book, came

[5] Lainey Greer, *Struggling with Body Image: Seeing What God Sees* (New Growth, 2024), 7.

from a series of lectures compiled in *Man and Woman He Created Them: A Theology of the Body*. The pope's fundamental questions drive his teaching and are meant to inform the Catholic faith. He asks, (1) How should God's children think about their bodies? and (2) Because God gave bodies as a gift to humanity, how are humans meant to treat their bodies? John Paul finds the answer to these questions in Christ's teaching in the Gospels. By seeing these teachings as definitive for humanity's origin, history, and destiny, Christ's followers can glean a foundational understanding of a theology of the body.[6]

In the evangelical world, some major contributions have come about in recent years. In *Embodied: Living as Whole People in a Fractured World*, Gregg R. Allison works through a biblical understanding of embodiment, examining the life of the physical body lived out in the world on a daily basis. Thus, Allison addresses the body in terms of creation, sex/gender, particularity, sociality, sexuality, incarnation, sanctification, blessing and discipline, worship, clothing, suffering and healing, death, and the future.

---

[6] John Paul II, *Man and Woman He Created Them: A Theology of the Body*, trans. Michael Waldstein (Pauline Books & Media, 2006), 460.

Each topic encompasses the importance of humanity's physical reality throughout the Bible, given that embodiment and doctrine overlap. Allison's first five chapters present the general framework for proper consideration of the body, with the application of that framework worked out in the rest of the book. The overall goal of his work is to help readers live as whole, embodied people in a fractured world.[7]

Timothy Tennent, in *For the Body: Recovering a Theology of Gender, Sexuality, and the Human Body*, develops his theology of the body to instruct believers on how to articulate what Christianity is *for* rather than what it stands *against*. Working through three sections, he first provides a Christian view of physical life founded on seven building blocks. Second, Tennent utilizes his proposed building blocks to confront errant cultural messages about the body. Third, he suggests ways the church can disciple others using his theology of the body, a concept that he rightly states is situated among the most pressing issues of our day.[8]

---

[7] Gregg R. Allison, *Embodied: Living as Whole People in a Fractured World* (Baker, 2021).

[8] Timothy C. Tennent, *For the Body: Recovering a Theology of Gender, Sexuality, and the Human Body* (Zondervan, 2020), xxii.

John Kleinig's *Wonderfully Made: A Protestant Theology of the Body* is the third example. Kleinig states at the outset that he offers a Protestant theology of the body—a welcome addition to the scant examples that currently exist on this topic. After laying the foundation for why the body matters, he moves into his proposal containing six aspects for a theology of the body: the created, redeemed, spiritual, sexual, spousal, and living body. His work is a helpful addition to the budding topic in Protestantism and works through categories similar to those of Tennent and Allison.[9]

While the aforementioned works have their unique contributions and strengths, I take a novel approach to a theology of the body, grounding it in the doctrine of God. As theological discussion begins with the doctrine of God, trinitarian involvement with the body offers the best foundation for a theology of the body. In fact, the apostle Paul lays out this trinitarian involvement in 1 Cor 6:12–20 by highlighting how the Father, Son, and Holy Spirit are each involved with the bodily experience of humanity. While nearly every doctrine implicates the body in various ways,

---

[9] John W. Kleinig, *Wonderfully Made: A Protestant Theology of the Body* (Lexham, 2021).

the starting point for our conception of the body should begin with the triune God.

From there, a second critical concept for the body arises: embodiment, or as it is often referred to, embodied reality. This view entails an understanding that God designed human beings as a simultaneous unity and duality. So, embodiment involves the constitution of a unified person who is distinctly immaterial soul and material body. Though disembodied for a time in the intermediate state, humans are both created and resurrected as embodied beings. Relatedly, the immaterial and material aspects of humanity interact and influence one another, revealing a divinely designed psychosomatic connection meant to enable and enhance human flourishing. Scripture attests to this mind and body interaction in verses such as Eccl 11:10 and 3 John 2. The connection is also evident in everyday examples, such as the way nervousness impacts the stomach or hunger affects emotions.

The reality of embodiment leads to the subsequent conclusion that both soul and body are valuable, each being a fundamental component of human existence.[10] With this

[10] These immaterial and material components of humanity are treated in the next chapter. To be clear, when referring

concept in place, the third and fourth layers involve practical realities that encompass the body's value—namely, body image and body stewardship. If the body matters to God and he commands us to glorify him in our bodies (see 1 Cor 6:20), then body image and body stewardship are the basic ways that command plays out in daily life.

The way we think about our bodies is known as "body image," and everyone has one. As our circumstances and bodies are ever-changing, most people will battle a negative body image. Still, the thoughts we hold about our bodies should glorify the God who created and will resurrect our bodies.[11] All Christians, no matter their age, sex,

---

to the soul and to spiritual capacities, I mean to encompass the thoughts of the mind and the feelings of the heart. These signs of immaterial existence make it clear that God designed humans as a united dualism where both soul and body are necessary for human flourishing. The embodied influence of immaterial on material and vice versa is understood as our psychosomatic (mind and body) connection that God created as an integral part of human experience. For more, from a neuroscientist, see Anthony Newberg and Mark Robert Waldman, *How God Changes Your Brain* (Ballantine, 2009); or, from a psychiatrist, see Bessel van der Kolk, *The Body Keeps the Score: Brain, Mind, and Body in the Healing of Trauma* (Penguin, 2015).

[11] For my full treatment on body image, see *Struggling with Body Image.*

physical impairments, or bodily hang-ups, should hold a God-honoring body image.

"Body stewardship" speaks to the way we treat our bodies, which is the other practical area of life where we should honor God. As the goal of this book is to convince you of embodied holiness, body stewardship is the underlying expectation that courses throughout. From the outset, it is critical to know that body stewardship involves accepting responsibility for the body by appropriately caring for its needs through proper nutrition, sufficient exercise, adequate rest, and stress management. We will unpack each one of these in chapters 5 and 6, which offer practical applications of the forthcoming biblical and theological chapters.

Body image and body stewardship are connected and naturally flow from a theology of the body and embodied reality. This recognition is the crux of the book. If we do not conceive of the body as valuable, we will not be concerned with its proper care. On the other hand, bodily neglect, harm, or misuse will not be fully rectified when misconceptions of the body persist. Therefore, we must have a solid understanding of the why before moving on to the what.

Theology of the Body: A Brief History

The trouble is that before Christians can assent to a biblical view of the body, we must relinquish erroneous views of it. Essentially, we must be convinced that the body matters. So, to develop a proper theology of the body, we first need to address an errant one. Paul, in his paramount example to the Corinthians that we will review, shows that such corrections were necessary to shift anti-body sentiments in the early church. This tendency continues today, as my brief, introductory story illustrates.[12] Ponder the following statements that emanate from a low and even adverse view of the body. While some may seem obvious, others are less overt. Still, each view elevates the soul over the body in one way or another.

---

[12] As Luke Timothy Johnson laments, this anti-body tendency is implicit in the lack of scholarship on the body. Luke Timothy Johnson, *The Revelatory Body: Theology as Inductive Art* (Eerdmans, 2015), 5. Still, this tendency can be explicit; Ola Sigurdson regards many Christians to be hostile toward the body in *Heavenly Bodies: Incarnation, the Gaze, and Embodiment in Christian Theology* (Eerdmans, 2016), 2. Though scholarship has grown in recent years, much work on a theology of the body remains to be done.

We have bodies, but we are souls.[13]
The fleshly body hinders the spiritual soul.[14]
Only your soul is from God.[15]
The body is a shell for the soul.[16]

---

[13] This conclusion is reminiscent of Aquinas, who held that, "the intellectual principle—or the soul—is the proper form of man." Thomas Aquinas, *Summa Theologica*, pt. 1, a. 76, art. 1. Because Aquinas adopted a valuation of soul over body, he "contributed to the ongoing disparagement of the human body and the elevation of the human soul in the church of the Middle Ages." Gregg R. Allison, *Historical Theology: An Introduction to Christian Doctrine* (Zondervan Academic, 2011), 330.

[14] This statement echoes Lactantius, who remarked that the "flesh hinders the spirit from following God." Lactantius, *The Divine Institutes* 4.25 (*ANF* 7:127). He went on to describe the body as evil, believing the separation of body from soul at death indicated that the "evil will perish and good be permanent." Lactantius, *Divine Institutes* 7.5 (*ANF*, 7:202).

[15] This thought reflects Cyprian, who described the soul as being from heaven while the body is from the earth. He lamented the tension between body and soul, believing a "daily . . . strife" existed between the two. Cyprian, *Treatise* 4.16 (*ANF* 5:451).

[16] This view perpetuates the influence of Platonic philosophy and was expressed in the early church as the body imprisoning the soul. *Letter to Diognetus* 6 (*ANF* 1:27). Watchman Nee similarly held that the body, or outward shell, houses the inner part of humanity that relates to God. Watchman Nee, *The Release of the Spirit* (Gospel Literature Service, 1965), 6.

Your soul is the real you.[17]

Christians are soul care physicians.[18]

---

[17] This line of thinking can be connected to heretical views that denied the Son of God would ever take on a full human nature, specifically the body. Teaching that Jesus only appeared human or that his body was in fact a "phantasm" and not of real, material substance not only distorted the gospel but also communicated the notion that personhood is only located in the soul. Ernest Evans, introduction to *Treatise on the Incarnation*, by Tertullian, ed. and trans. Ernest Evans (SPCK, 1956), xxvii.

[18] This phrase is often heard in biblical and Christian counseling circles. Though a necessary sentiment, it can render the counselee's soul paramount. Even without an expressed negativity toward the body, it communicates an importance of the soul that is not extended to the body. Often, engaging in wellness basics like adequate sleep, proper nutrition, and sufficient exercise can positively impact one's mental health. Counselors don't need expertise in these wellness areas, but simply inquiring about a counselee's health habits is a great start. Thus, this language furthers the elevation of soul over body, as does the popular phrase, embodied souls. Because "embodiment" communicates the dual reality of an immaterial and material being, "embodied soul" still highlights soul over body. While this designation may seem innocuous and less anti-body than the others, it is a double emphasis on the soul: soul + body = soul. If Christians are to correct any misconceptions about soul and body, our common terminology must undergo sufficient scrutiny.

You may have heard these phrases in the church, at a conference, or from a trusted organization, or you may even have uttered them yourself. When spoken, they often go unchallenged because Christians are used to a pious version of Christianity that divorces the physical from the spiritual. Perhaps one final example will be convincing. Consider the verses of the beloved hymn often sung at funerals, "I'll Fly Away": In the first verse, the songwriter contends that when his life on earth is over, he will blissfully fly away to his heavenly home. In the second, he states that after he has passed through all of life's gloom, he will be like a caged bird set free. And in still another, he rejoices that one day he will have never-ending joy; he needs only to endure the few tiring days of his life that remain.[19]

This hymn communicates the same anti-body message: that the real you, presently shut up behind prison bars, will be finally set free at death. While we do long for an eternity unencumbered by the impact of sin, our forever existence will not be bodiless. So, Christians should fight to affirm the body. As this book will argue,

---

[19] See Albert E. Brumley, "I'll Fly Away" (1929), Popular Hymns.com, https://popularhymns.com/ill-fly-away.

the believer's body is a temple of the Spirit, not a tomb for the soul.[20]

Because of that reality, while not elevating the body over the soul or physical matters over spiritual ones, this book naturally focuses on the body. Discussion of an embodied holiness assumes the soul's involvement. The correction that Christians must make is to include the body's involvement—to be wholly holy, sanctified completely, fully blameless in our spirit, soul, and body (1 Thess 5:23). This task demands bringing our understanding of the body in alignment with the emphasis we have long placed on the soul. While space does not permit

---

[20] I will highlight the reason for much of this thinking in chapter 2, which discusses anti-body philosophies such as Platonism, Gnosticism, and asceticism. Streams of Christianity have long regarded "the body as though it were shameful, worthless, or unimportant." Nancy R. Pearcey, *Love Thy Body: Answering Hard Questions About Life and Sexuality* (Baker Books, 2018), 9. Though some would push back against Christians being characterized as occasionally anti-body, if nothing else, the logical conclusion is that we have, at times, suppressed the body's significance. John Cooper sees this suppression as a detriment to Christian orthopraxy, an assertion I hope to convince you of in this book. John W. Cooper, *Body, Soul, and Life Everlasting: Biblical Anthropology and the Monism-Dualism Debate* (Eerdmans, 2000), 26.

it here, I have given significant attention to inaccurate beliefs Christians hold about the body in another work.[21] For now, a couple of examples will suffice.

Misconstruing the apostle Paul's view of the body is a significant contributor to a flawed assumption of corporeal existence today. Take the Greek word *sarx*, meaning "flesh." One meaning refers to sinful nature, but another meaning is a neutral reference to the flesh of one's body or the body itself. Failure to recognize alternate meanings of *sarx* can lead to a dismissive take on corporeity (the quality of having a physical body), at least one that reckons the body to be the sole source of sin. Consider 2 Cor 4:10–11 as an example of a neutral, and even positive, emphasis

---

[21] Some such inaccuracies Christians struggle with are the following: We misapply the image of God to the soul and not the body. We view holiness as a spiritual pursuit that is hindered by physical matters. We miss the full promise of glorification. We forget that just as Christ took on a body in the incarnation, he remains embodied. We are confused about the meaning of *sarx*, the Greek word for "flesh." We misconstrue Paul's statement in 1 Tim 4:8 that physical training is only of some value. We make conclusions about the body based on individual views read apart from context. We assume the body's insignificance based on its temporary separation from the soul. Greer, *Struggling with Body Image*, 35–37.

on the flesh. Here Paul goes out of his way to show that *sarx*, the flesh, does not always refer to one's sinful nature. In 4:10, he states that believers carry the death of Jesus in the body (*sōma*, Paul's most common word for body) so that the life of Jesus may also be manifested in our bodies (*sōma*). But in the subsequent verse, he repeats himself, this time using *sarx* instead of *sōma*. If Christians can manifest the life of Jesus in our *sarx*, or flesh, as we do in our *sōma*, or body, then we recognize that not every New Testament instance of the flesh implies a negative connection between the body and sinful nature.

Another misunderstanding happens when one cites a singular text from Paul to prove the body's insignificance, which inaccurately reflects his entire corpus on the body. In Romans 7, he articulates a battle between the law of his mind versus the law of sin dwelling in his members, seeking deliverance from his body (*sōma*) of death. A quick reading of this text in isolation could lead one to assume the body is the source of sin against the sinless mind (7:22–25). But, as we should do with all Scripture, when we read this passage in context, specifically with chapters 6 and 8, we get a fuller picture of Paul's teaching on the body. Chapter 6 shows that Christians can present this same body's members to God. Being brought from death to life, we use the parts of our body for righteousness (6:12–14). Then, following his confession in chapter 7, Paul teaches in chapter 8 that the Spirit has given life to our mortal bodies. Even more, he communicates an already/not-yet aspect of our adoption as God's children through Christ by the Spirit. Paul proclaims that adoption (in essence, salvation) will not be complete until our bodies are redeemed. So, we reckon that the body of sin and death is also the body of righteousness and life that will be fully redeemed (8:11, 23).

If Christians are to comprehend an embodied view of holiness, biblical concepts matter. If Scripture addresses the body, God specially designs our bodies, and he expects us to glorify him in those bodies, then our beliefs should influence our lifestyles. Thus, the believer's view and stewardship of the body are key aspects of embodied holiness.

Cultural Pendulum

Before going any further, let us pause to determine our cultural context. Christians desperately need to hold to a biblical view of the body, living out an embodied holiness amid a culture that knows nothing of a Christian worldview and holds unbiblical conceptions of the body. For Christians to distinguish ourselves from the world, we must recognize what we are up against as it pertains to bodily existence.

The culture's take on the body swings back and forth like the swing of a pendulum from idolizing the body to ignoring the body, and Christians need wisdom to avoid such pendulum swings. To start, we must recognize that the culture presses for disembodied living on either end of the pendulum. Disembodied living means seeking to function in ways that oppose God's design of embodiment. We are unified beings, distinctly immaterial soul and material body, with a psychosomatic connection. Disembodiment involves a choice to live as though one of the aspects of human composition holds no bearing on the other—to function as though the material is paramount and the immaterial is a waste of time, or as though immaterial existence demands such focus that disregard for the material results. Either way, it means going against the way God designed us to exist. And in the end, neither extreme will work, as the mind and body are meant to influence one another. Consider the following examples.

An idolatrous embrace of the body reflects much of what can be seen scrolling social media. The body is all that matters. The pursuit of outward perfection is paramount, through obsessive exercise, strict eating regimens, plastic surgeries, workout routines, the finest clothing, the best hair and skin products, adherence to beauty trends, the right influencers, and the spending of every resource on getting better, looking better, and being better. The problem is that this self-focused lifestyle distracts from pursuing whatever lies outside of self, namely, the Creator God to whom all will one day give an account. A lifestyle like this elevates the body and dismisses soul. This way of living is devoted to the here and now, without being weighed down by the thought of what is to come.

Similarly, when so much focus gets put on physical health, mental health—another essential reality of immaterial existence—gets overlooked. This disembodied living will not work either, as two quick examples will make clear. Think about the ways physical health was prioritized during the COVID pandemic. Protecting the body and immune system was paramount, so we "social distanced," remained at home, stayed away from loved ones, masked our faces, and met virtually. But as the statistics now reveal, that sole focus on physical health came with a detrimental impact on mental health.[22] Or, relatedly, consider the toll

---

[22] John Gramlich, "Mental Health and the Pandemic: What US Surveys Have Found," Pew Research Center, March 2, 2023,

an abortion has on the mother. We are told that aborting a baby is just a healthcare decision, and that, as pro-choice supporters advocate, abortions should be celebrated. But many mothers who chose abortion battle ongoing mental and emotional anguish.[23] And this is not just from terminating a life inside of them. It is also because the act of

---

https://www.pewresearch.org/short-reads/2023/03/02/mental-health-and-the-pandemic-what-u-s-surveys-have-found/. Sadly, much of the increase in depression and anxiety has been recorded among young adults.

[23] Vincent M. Rue et al., "Induced Abortion and Traumatic Stress: A Preliminary Comparison of American and Russian Women," *Medical Science Monitor* 10, no. 10 (2004): SR5–16. Though conducted in the early 2000s, this well-known study continues to inform our understanding of abortion and mental health today. Importantly, Rue found that 65 percent of women who had an abortion experienced symptoms of PTSD and 60 percent admitted feeling as if part of them had died. These findings alone are evidence of embodiment, that a physiological action performed in the body bears a psychological consequence in the mind. Another study found that post-abortion mothers were at an elevated risk of substance abuse, turning to drugs and alcohol to numb the mind and body. Additionally, they also experienced an increased risk of suicide. D. M. Fergusson et al., "Abortion and Mental Health Disorders: Evidence from a 30-Year Longitudinal Study," *British Journal of Psychiatry* 193, no. 6 (2008): 444–51, http://doi.org/10.1192/bjp.bp.108.056499.

abortion is more than a medical operation; it is a physiological procedure that often comes with lasting psychological impact. In both examples, immaterial realities suffer when we treat them as less important than material ones.

Then, with a swing of the pendulum, comes a society that ignores the body. It is one that champions an autonomous existence despite anatomical realities, where the creature can become his own creator. The transgender movement presents the foremost example of disembodied living. For someone questioning his or her gender identity, experts recommend transitioning.[24] The body is medicated and mutilated, while feelings are elevated and protected. Biological realities mean nothing; they can be altered to align with mental imaginations. While this attempt to function in such a disembodied way is touted as the only answer, studies reveal the detrimental results.[25]

---

[24] To understand the pressure to transition, read Pamela Paul, "As Kids, They Thought They Were Trans. They No Longer Do," *New York Times*, February 2, 2024, https://www.nytimes.com/2024/02/02/opinion/transgender-care.html.

[25] "Doctors Protecting Children Declaration," Doctors Protecting Children, https://doctorsprotectingchildren.org/. Incidentally, as I noted in *Struggling with Body Image*, gender dysphoria is the only condition in which one's mental distortions

Another consideration is the heightened focus on mental health and working through "traumas." We are quickly becoming a culture so obsessed with discussing our mental health that we are in danger of dismissing our physical health. The media, from commercials to social media, podcasters to influencer trends, bombard us with the prioritization of mental health. And while mental health does matter, in a country facing rising rates of obesity and chronic disease, physical health does too, especially as one impacts the other.[26]

Standing Firm

In the current of cultural confusion, Christians must stand firm on the goodness of embodied reality and

---

are encouraged and supported. Anorexics are not told to continue starving themselves; bulimics are not given laxatives; bigorexics are not supplied with steroids, and sufferers from body dysmorphic disorder are not provided plastic surgery. However, dysphoria that focuses on genitalia is fostered and upheld. One has to wonder why. Greer, *Struggling with Body Image*, 28–29.

[26] "Obesity," The Nutrition Source, Harvard T. H. Chan School of Public Health, https://nutritionsource.hsph.harvard.edu/obesity/.

God's intention behind creating body and soul, male and female image-bearers, full of dignity and purpose. Maleness and femaleness are fundamental givens of human existence. In existence as an embodied person, gender is an essential piece of embodiment. Today, however, culture often disregards the creation event, biological gender, and embodied humanity. Society's message is that you can dictate your own embodied experience. This desire to be other than your created self is rooted in a fundamental denial of God—God as Creator and determiner of all things. It is an idolatrous endeavor to become your own god.

Thus, the church must stand firm on the biblical truths of God creating humans as man and woman (Gen 1:26–28), God weaving each human together as man or woman purposefully and specifically in his or her mother's womb (Psalm 139), Christ incarnating as an embodied male and not in an ambiguous human existence (John 1:14), and God intentionally placing men and women in the exact time and space he wanted so that they would come to know him (Acts 17:24–28). Scripture attests to these foundational realities of embodied existence, and a sound theology of the body affirms these truths.

As embodied beings, Christians are commanded to glorify God in our bodies (1 Cor 6:20) and called to obedience in spiritual and physical matters. Still, the tendency has often been to misunderstand embodiment, which manifests in an elevation of the soul and a devaluation of the body. This hierarchical thinking surfaces in behaviors that downplay the body's worth—a long-standing issue with gnostic roots that Paul tackled in the Corinthian church. His countermeasure against the licentious behaviors of these anti-body believers was to highlight trinitarian involvement with the body. This view was meant to correct misconceptions about the body's value and provide a foundation that prescribed God-honoring behaviors. In essence, Paul went after their actions by correcting their thoughts.

By this same foundation today, believers can correct body-neglecting behaviors within the church, not to mention address the culture's simultaneous body-denying beliefs and body-worshipping ideals by living differently in a disembodied world.

With these fundamental components in place, I can now preview the book's outline, which unfolds in four arguments before turning to applicable content designed to show the way of embodied holiness.

Chapter Outline

In chapter 1, on a biblical argument for the body, an overview of Scripture will demonstrate that the body and health cannot be neglected in the pursuit of embodied holiness. For the believer, whose embodied life should be devoted to the glory of God, spirituality cannot be pursued apart from physicality. In a culture that in many ways denies the goodness of physical realities, believers cannot afford to do the same.

An anthropological argument for the body in chapter 2 will address the reality that God created humanity in his image as material and immaterial men and women. Because we bear the *imago Dei* as embodied beings, this distinguishing characteristic reflects a psychosomatic connection that cannot be deconstructed to elevate soul over body. We were specifically designed to carry out the creation commands of procreation and vocation, which require embodiment and solidify the value of soul and body. However, when embodiment is misunderstood and our psychosomatic connection is not protected, neglect of the body and physical health naturally follows.

Chapter 3, a theological argument for the body, will argue that the triune God affirms the body in a variety of ways—namely, in the divine acts of creation, redemption, indwelling, and resurrection. To argue for the body's value, the apostle Paul highlights this trinitarian involvement with the body to an audience highly influenced by Gnosticism, exemplified in their anti-body thinking and acting. I will argue that 1 Cor 6:12–20 serves as the ultimate text to connect how Christians think about their bodies with the way they treat them.

The fourth chapter will provide a historical argument for the body that will show how believers have historically recognized the connection between holiness and corporeity. From various creeds, to the seven deadly sins and the *Westminster Larger Catechism*, it will be clear that some Christian forebearers understood why the body's condition was an important link in allowing our orthodoxy to determine our orthopraxy.

The fifth chapter will offer wellness basics meant as a guide to bodily care specific to the four areas of body stewardship: exercise, nutrition, rest, and stress management. Each one is vital, as they correspond to how God designed our bodies.

The sixth chapter will assess current evidence on the way Christians presently view and treat their bodies and end with final admonitions from Scripture. Though these are difficult subjects, to rectify any misunderstandings of the body, we must be first apprised of these realities.

Finally, the book will conclude with a fresh vision for glorifying God in our bodies, along with a list of personal questions to consider for an embodied holiness.

1

A Biblical Argument for the Body

Since we have these promises, beloved, let us cleanse ourselves from every defilement of body and spirit, bringing holiness to completion in the fear of God" (2 Cor 7:1). Out of reverent devotion to God, Christians pursue an embodied holiness, one that seeks spiritual and physical cleansing only brought to completion in Christ.

While not meant as an exhaustive commentary on biblical references to the body, this section surveys the body's significance discussed throughout the pages of Scripture. The passages compel a deeper understanding of bodily life, one that acknowledges its importance to the Christian faith. Additional texts will be examined in subsequent chapters, as their foci—while pertaining to the body—bring greater clarity to related arguments in this book.

Old Testament

From the outset, it is obvious that twenty-first-century life is vastly different from that of the early centuries when both testaments were penned. Unimaginable differences exist between our lifestyles and those of Joseph, Ruth, or Barnabas. With modern technologies and conveniences available, Christians should ask themselves if the ease of living has brought about a complacent faith, one where certain areas of life are overlooked? For instance, how do the choices we make from convenience and busyness impact our health? As with all other questions in life, God's Word remains the perfect guide to provide us answers. Turning to the Old Testament, we reflect on what it means to express an embodied holiness, loving God with all our hearts, souls, minds, and strength.

References to the body's importance are found throughout the Old Testament, and while several texts could be examined, our focus will mainly be Genesis 1–2, as it sets the foundation for a biblical view of physical life. Before moving to the New Testament, a summary of embodied language throughout Wisdom literature will show the Israelites emphasized the totality of humankind.

Genesis 1:26–28; 2:7–8

> *Then God said, "Let us make man in our image, after our likeness. And let them have dominion over the fish of the sea and over the birds of the heavens and over the livestock and over all the earth and over every creeping thing that creeps on the earth." So God created man in his own image, in the image of God he created him; male and female he created them. And God blessed them. And God said to them, "Be fruitful and multiply and fill the earth and subdue it and have dominion over the fish of the sea and over the birds of the heavens and over every living thing that moves on the earth."*
>
> *. . . Then the* Lord *God formed the man of dust from the ground and breathed into his nostrils the breath of life, and the man became a living creature. And the* Lord *God planted a garden in Eden, in the east, and there he put the man whom he had formed.*

A brief reading of Gen 1:26–28 communicates that all humanity is made in God's image. Humans are specifically suited to bear God's image as spiritual and physical beings, conferring dignity to both soul and body. Plainly understood, we depict the *imago Dei* as embodied human beings. While there is much conjecture on what imaging God entails, I prefer a holistic understanding of humans as God's embodied image-bearers, which encompasses spiritual, substantive, ethical, relational, and functional views. Rather than the image existing only in one aspect of human existence, who we are as whole beings—able to commune with God, rationalize, express moral choices, engage in relationships, and exert dominion over creation—combines to holistically represent God. Instead of putting limitations on this dignified distinction, such a view proclaims the depths of how God created his embodied image-bearers who both spiritually and physically express the *imago Dei*.

Moreover, the text does not specify image-bearing to one aspect of our being over the other—namely, by locating the image in soul over body. No scriptural evidence can be found for splitting up and parsing out the *imago Dei*.[1]

---

[1] Gentry and Wellum understand that the image of God implies a structural element, which is clearly the body.

To constrain image-bearing to the soul as opposed to the body is neo-gnostic, valuing the spiritual and devaluing the physical.[2] It is to press for an ascetic piety that partitions the faith, rendering anything tangible or material as inconsequential. Ultimately, it presents a confounded Christian faith regarding eschatological realities of the new heavens, new earth, and resurrected, reembodied believers who will be bodily transformed like the glorious body of Christ.

Essential Components. One of those important introductory concepts is God's creative activity on the

---

Peter J. Gentry and Stephen J. Wellum, *Kingdom Through Covenant: A Biblical and Theological Understanding of the Covenants*, 2nd ed. (Crossway, 2018), 192. Such an acknowledgment is critical, as Berkouwer explains, "Theologians, in their search for the meaning of the image, often sought various similarities or analogies between God and man, without thereby giving up the difference between God and man. In the search for such analogies, it often happened that man's body was excluded from the image of God." G. C. Berkouwer, *Man: The Image of God* (Eerdmans, 1952), 71.

[2] While Gnosticism will be explained in the next chapter, at this point it is essential to know it is a belief system that views the material realm as evil, which implicates the body and destroys its value.

sixth day.[3] The creation of man is the pinnacle of all his works, evidenced in that human beings are the only creations esteemed by his image and likeness (Gen 1:26–27). According to Peter Gentry, image and likeness are best summarized as representing sonship and rulership, which both involve the body.[4] For humans to fulfill their roles as sons and rulers, they require both spiritual and physical capacities; thus, the body cannot be separated from image and likeness.[5]

---

[3] Quinn and Greeson also recognize the importance of the body to the *imago Dei*. And pertinent to this book's content, they too understand that "Christian discipline and self-care should attend the whole person." Benjamin T. Quinn and Dennis T. Greeson, *The Way of Christ in Culture: A Vision for All of Life* (B&H Academic, 2024) 73.

[4] Peter J. Gentry, "Kingdom Through Covenant: Humanity as the Divine Image," *The Southern Baptist Journal of Theology* 12, no. 1 (2008): 12.

[5] The image of God is central to Bavinck's anthropology. He understands the difference between soul and body alongside the dependence of soul and body. He finds that it is "helpful to conceive of human persons as having at once a spiritual and material, supernatural and natural, super sensory and sensory, heavenly and earthly, eternal and temporal side." Herman Bavinck, *Reformed Ethics*, vol. 1, *Created, Fallen, and Converted Humanity*, ed. and trans. John Bolt (Baker Academic, 2019), 44.

Further details of this apex event are given in Genesis 2 when God forms man from the dust of the ground, breathing into him the breath of life. Dust and breath coalesce; the man becomes a living being (Gen 2:7) and is blessed by God as a fully formed human (Gen 1:28). Adam from the *adama* (Hebrew text) is constructed of both spiritual and physical aspects, unified but distinct.[6] He is not only made to experience a relationship with his Creator spiritually but also to fulfill his Creator's commands physically, existing as an embodied being. In sum, both soul and body are essential human, image-bearing components.[7]

---

[6] Joshua Farris understands that

> the author of Genesis 2 describes humans as composed in some way of the dust of the ground and indicates that the life that is given is given to the body to make it alive. The "breath" spoken of can be naturally read in light of the larger canon of Scripture as the soul that God creates and is unique highlighted in contrast to the rest of God's creation, signifying the fact that God is adding something new.

Joshua R. Farris, *An Introduction to Theological Anthropology: Humans, Both Creaturely and Divine* (Baker Academic, 2020), 20.

[7] G. C. Berkouwer agrees, saying, "Scripture's emphasis on the whole man as the image of God has triumphed time and time again over all objections and opposing principles.

A Garden Attendant. At the end of the creation event, God took a rest day from his life-giving activity, not because he required it, but to establish the principle of rest for his finite beings and enjoy his handiwork on previous days. Before the formation of the male and female image-bearers, the more detailed creation narrative in Genesis 2 explains that no plants had sprung from the ground, as God had not yet brought rain. Plants require tending, and there was no man to work the ground or cultivate the foliage that grew from the earth.[8] God's magnificent garden would need a caretaker (Gen 2:4–15). With his material world constructed, a material being must keep it, a being imbued with the Creator's image to best attend to his

---

Scripture never makes a distinction between man's spiritual and bodily attributes to limit the image of God to the spiritual, as furnishing the only possible analogy between man and God." Berkouwer, *Man*, 77.

[8] I am not saying the sole or paramount reason humanity was created was to render care for creation. While humans are to be stewards of nature, they were ultimately created for a relationship with their Creator. As Acts 17:24–28 reveals, throughout history, every person has been sovereignly designed and placed in a divinely determined, exact time and space so that each image-bearing human might reach out and find God, who is their source of life.

creation. Physical maintenance requires physical existence, as this essential part of the creation narrative explains.[9]

Creation Commands. In the creation commands, humans are tasked with authority and responsibility, thus

[9] I appreciate the way Bavinck articulates humanity's "relation to nature" regarding how God's image-bearing creatures connect with the created world. Bavinck, *Reformed Ethics*, 61–62. While the New Age Movement misconstrues much of God's good design for his created world, Christians can affirm the incredible ways nature impacts us as embodied beings. I refer to such benefits as embodied interventions, which "are effective because of our immaterial and material design. God mediates care to believers through these embodied interventions. He comforts us, giving us a mind of peace that quiets anxieties as we engage in his world through our bodies. When pursued to deepen our relationship with God, these physical actions come with spiritual blessing. . . . God designed the natural world to declare his glory and to renew our perspective as we take a break from mundane routines and get into his awe-inspiring, created world, a world filled with natural blessings that benefit our immune and nervous systems along with overall cellular health. Get outside, soak up the sun, put your feet and hands in the grass, sand, or dirt, play with a pet, listen to the birds, flowing water, wind, and other soothing sounds in God's glorious creation." Lainey Greer, "Feeling Anxious? Use Your Body to Calm Your Mind," Your Body Matters, September 4, 2024, https://laineygreer.com/feeling-anxious-use-your-body-to-calm-your-mind/.

positioned over the rest of creation as their Creator expresses authority and responsibility over them (Psalm 8). Dominion is to be expressed over everything in the sea and all the creeping things on the earth, and this expression occurs bodily. Just as material plants and animals are an integral part of the creation narrative, material human beings are even more indispensable, serving as ongoing, physical representations of the One who holds ultimate dominion.

Part of conveying that God-given dominion involves carrying out the commands to be fruitful, to multiply, to fill the earth, and to subdue it. The first humans are responsible for growing their numbers and spreading out over all creation to continue the multiplying-subduing-stewarding task as God's embodied image-bearers. The actualization of these commands requires physical life, as manifesting dominion through procreation and vocation transpires via the material world through tangible bodies. The need for physical existence in fulfilling God's creation commands is evident. Image-bearing, embodied beings and the creation commands are intertwined for the full experience and actualization of human flourishing.[10]

---

[10] Flourishing, from the Greek *eudaimonia*, can also mean soul happiness and expresses the natural drive of all mankind to

These opening chapters of Scripture reveal the requisite physicality of humanity, which demands more than an obligatory admission that the body is part of the image of God; it requires wholehearted confession that physical constitution is just as essential as spiritual capacity. Thus, these passages provide a meaningful foundation to the argument associating physical health with holiness. If our bodies are embedded with the significance of the *imago Dei*, then surely Christians should recognize the inherent responsibility of bodily care as part of a devoted life lived in praise of the One who purposefully designed us as embodied spiritual, physical beings.[11]

---

seek happiness. As beings created to glorify God and enjoy him forever, the ultimate experience of flourishing necessitates the ability to enjoy life via a body. Johnathan Pennington, *Jesus the Great Philosopher: Rediscovering the Wisdom Needed for the Good Life* (Brazos, 2020), 187.

[11] For more on the image of God, see John F. Kilner, *Dignity and Destiny: Humanity in the Image of God* (Eerdmans, 2015); Craig G. Bartholomew and Michael W. Goheen, *The Drama of Scripture: Finding Our Place in the Biblical Story* (Baker Academic, 2024); Vaughan Roberts, *God's Big Picture: Tracing the Storyline of the Bible* (InterVarsity, 2003); Michael D. Williams, *Far As the Curse Is Found: The Covenant Story of Redemption* (P&R, 2005).

Wisdom Literature

The frequent use of embodiment language is seen throughout Wisdom literature. God does not want us to suffer from the consequences of sin in our souls or bodies. Christians are meant to live wisely, to experience an embodied existence freed from the effects of sin, though this will not be fully realized in this life. Wisdom literature depicts sin's impact on body and soul, while also commending righteous choices that benefit both soul and body. A brief overview of these examples demonstrates the depth of embodiment language throughout this Old Testament genre.

Consider David as he flees his enemies, feeling an embodied grief of intense anguish in soul and body (Ps 31:6–10). When bearing the consequences of his sinful choices, David feels as if his bones waste away while his strength is sapped (Ps 32:3–5). Another psalmist carries the weight of affliction in his bones, heart, and skin (Ps 102:1–11). He struggles to sleep from the effects of God's wrath because, as the biblical authors explain, grief vexes the heart, and evil troubles the body (Ps 102:1–11; Eccl 11:10).

Conversely, we enjoy the blessings of godly living as embodied beings. One psalmist experiences a deep, all-consuming desire for God, feeling it as an embodied being whose soul and flesh cries out for the Lord (Ps 84:2). Psalms 119:73 and 139:13–14 break out in praise to the Lord for the body.[12] David details how God fearfully and wonderfully made his body, forming and knitting his inward parts in his mother's womb. Praising God for the intricacies of his physical frame, David exemplifies a deep recognition of and appreciation for the body. Both the formation of the body and its physicality are significant. Believers should marvel at the body's construction. So, on the way to embodied holiness, we confess and glorify God for his intentional and magnificent design of the body, no matter its condition, form, or functional abilities.[13]

---

[12] For a more detailed examination of Ps 139:13–16, see Lainey Greer, *Struggling with Body Image: Seeing What God Sees* (New Growth, 2024), 12–13.

[13] A thoroughgoing theology of the body speaks to impaired, physical abilities and offers unique hope for disabled people. Being either able-bodied or disabled is largely temporary. For Christians who experience physical impairments, these will be eternally and permanently rectified in the new heaven and earth. And many people who are currently able-bodied will face disability at some point in life, whether from injury or age-related decline. For that reason, recognizing the dignity of embodied beings, no matter their physical ability, is critical to a Christian worldview. The theology of the body presented in this

Proverbs calls for the display of wisdom in all areas of life, including corporeal actions, a definite reality that is integral to embodied holiness. Solomon teaches this concept outright, saying that a wise life begins with rightly fearing the Lord and avoiding evil. From this foundation, the body receives health and nourishment (Prov 3:7–8). Rather than a disembodied approach to wise living that focuses only on the spiritual, proper fear of the Lord elicits a whole-person pursuit that produces embodied benefits.

A chapter later, in Prov 4:20–27, Solomon unlocks the key to obedience lived out through the body. First, he calls his son to hear his teaching and the words of wisdom that come from the Lord, for obedience brings life and healing to the body. Second, Solomon explains the body's involvement in keeping the commands of Scripture. Using bodily terminology, Solomon explains how his son can avoid sin and destruction through the wise application of the Word in all areas of life. Just as wisdom brings life and health to our body, it guards our hearts, keeps our lips from crooked speech, and sets our eyes forward to seek sure paths for our

---

book, with its emphasis on creation, incarnation, and indwelling in a later chapter, presents a special hope for believers with physical impairments.

feet (Prov 4:20–27).[14] While life is cut short due to foolish and wicked choices, proper fear of God lengthens our days (Prov 10:27). Anxiety weighs on the heart, but a peaceful heart brings life to our flesh, as pleasant words heal both soul and body (Prov 12:25; 14:30; 16:24). And thankfully, if a crushed spirit dries up our bones, a joyful heart serves as good medicine (Prov 17:22).

While brief, these introductory texts from the Old Testament, particularly Genesis 1–2, reveal God's intentionality in designing his image-bearers with spiritual and physical capabilities meant to enable their flourishing as embodied beings.

New Testament

Now we turn to the New Testament for a greater understanding of the body's value, which is a declaration critical to including physical health as part of embodied holiness. Like the previous section, this one does not present an exhaustive overview of Scripture but rather highlights passages that are most convincing of the body's significance.

---

[14] Greer, "The Utilization of a Theology of Human Embodiment to Address Body Image," 28.

Interestingly, the apostle Paul penned most of the following verses. The frequency of his writing on the body stands out, and his reason is profound. He proclaims that the pursuit of holiness is an embodied endeavor, thus his emphasis on the body in these verses. A natural conclusion from his writing is that he reckons humans as soul and body beings, called to fully devote themselves to God. Additionally, his discussion of physical existence, what he said about it, and whom he addressed are essential elements in the biblical promotion of physical health. Because his argument to the anti-body Corinthians is central to my theology of the body, the most significant text of Paul's corporeal focus, 1 Cor 6:12–20, will resume in the next chapter. For now, we begin with a brief note on Christ's anthropology.

Matthew 10:28

> *"And do not fear those who kill the body but cannot kill the soul. Rather fear him who can destroy both soul and body in hell."*

In Matt 10:28, Jesus declares that humans are soul-and-body beings and subject to almighty God. As immaterial and material beings, humans are ultimately accountable to their Creator, who retains authority over physical and spiritual death. Even if threatened with painful death in the present life, believers trust in God's sovereignty over both temporal and eternal life. This truth is vital to an embodied view of holiness. It reminds sinful humans who naturally oppose their Creator that even the body lies within the jurisdiction of the One who made all things. Therefore, the whole of one's life, in soul and body, must be lived before God in reverent fear. If the soul matters, so does the body.

Romans 6:12–13

> *Let not sin therefore reign in your mortal body, to make you obey its passions. Do not present your members to sin as instruments for unrighteousness, but present yourselves to God as those who have been brought from death to life, and your members to God as instruments for righteousness.*

In Rom 6:12–13, Paul confirms that sanctification is a bodily event that requires participation of the whole being.[15] If the body is a conduit of sinful action, then upon redemption it can be devoted to God as a conduit of righteous behavior. The command not to let sin reign in the body infers the converse—that sin naturally *does* reign in the fallen body (and soul). Paul's command for believers to not present the body's members to sin indicates that the normal occurrence in a fallen world is bodily disobedience. But the remedy is not disdain for the body. The command speaks to a depth of depravity that affects every part of the human being. So, Christians understand humanity's need for comprehensive renewal, one that is spiritual and physical, of soul and of body. In Christ and by the power of the Spirit, believers can choose not to let sin reign in their bodies.

Even more, God bids Christians to live an active faith. The commands of holy living pertain to cognitive,

---

[15] Bavinck argues for this very concept: "From now on we offer the members of our body and the self as instruments of righteousness (Rom. 6:13) to God unto sanctification (v. 19). . . . That is to say: the entire organism of our personality (soul, spirit, body, etc.) must be an instrument of righteousness, governed by the Spirit and not by the flesh." Bavinck, *Reformed Ethics*, 349. This recognition is the language of embodiment. God desires obedience from the whole person loving the Lord with all one's heart, soul, mind, and strength (Deut 6:4–5; Mark 12:30–31).

affectual, and behavioral obedience. Each play out via the body based on the desire of the soul. Determination of the body, not only intention of the soul, serves as a critical component in the fight for holiness.

Romans 12:1–2

> *I appeal to you therefore, brothers, by the mercies of God, to present your bodies as a living sacrifice, holy and acceptable to God, which is your spiritual worship. Do not be conformed to this world, but be transformed by the renewal of your mind, that by testing you may discern what is the will of God, what is good and acceptable and perfect.*

Owing to God's incredible mercies explained in the preceding eleven chapters, Romans 12 begins with a charge to believers to present their whole selves to God and avoids the compartmentalization of faith to merely spiritual matters. Paul specifically links body and soul, stating the surrender of the body is a manifestation of spiritual worship.

Because of everything the Father accomplished for us by Christ through the Spirit, believers surrender their whole selves, presenting their bodies to the Lord as a spiritual act of worship. Thus, faithful obedience in the Christian life is not limited to spiritual realities alone. The body is also to be given to God in holiness. God is glorified in the surrender of our embodied existence because it involves the deliberate decision to give back to him that which already belongs to him.

Paul does not stop with the body but includes the mind, calling for it to likewise be renewed by the truth of God's Word.[16] Like the body, the mind requires renewal because embodied beings are impacted by sin both spiritually and physically. But, also like the body, the mind can be transformed and devoted to God. A yielded embodied experience stands in contrast to the world, as it is driven by transformed thinking lived out in one's corporeity.[17]

---

[16] The next chapter considers the influence of Gnosticism on Christian beliefs regarding the body, but Paul combats early forms of gnostic thought in the New Testament. His point here communicates that the mind is not some pure, uncorruptible aspect dissimilar to the body. It is the whole, embodied being, in mind and body, that should be devoted to God, not given to sin.

[17] In these verses, Grudem also estimates that believers should aim to present themselves to the Lord as spiritually and physically healthy: "Our physical health is important. So we should take reasonable care of our bodies to make them effective instruments for the Holy Spirit to work through in this life. The

Being redeemed, the embodied believer is responsible for a submitted body and mind in response to God's incredible mercies. In this sense, as much as it lies within our control, the condition of the body is relevant. We must ask ourselves, What does it mean to be holy and acceptable before the Lord, specifically bodily?[18]

Lastly, it may seem curious that Paul deems our physical surrender to God a reasonable act of worship, but his intention is clear. He does not bifurcate spiritual and physical surrender to make a point about one versus the other. Rather, his purpose is to communicate that embodied believers—who are distinctly body and soul and yet intertwined physically and spiritually—should offer themselves to God in the entirety of their being. Therefore,

---

strength of our bodies is something that we can present to God as an offering to be used in service to him." Wayne Grudem, *Christian Ethics: An Introduction to Biblical Moral Reasoning* (Crossway, 2018), 657.

[18] Given my background with anorexia, I can attest to having little concern for surrender, let alone whether or not God was pleased with the condition of my body. Not until I experienced the Spirit's heavy hand of conviction did I give any thought to surrendering my sinful desires to the Lord. It was then that I could begin to assess the devotion of my whole embodied self.

an embodied view of holiness understands that the body should be offered as a sacrificial act that pleases God.

1 Corinthians 10:31

> *So, whether you eat or drink, or whatever you do, do all to the glory of God.*

Paul gives an overarching command to the anti-body Corinthians that extends to all believers. Glorifying God in whatever you do requires examining all actions, even mindless, everyday activities. Devoting everything—inherently one's embodied self—to God means living a life of worship wherein all thinking, believing, desiring, acting, speaking, and behaving should be God-honoring. When every aspect of who you are and what you do is spent for the glory of God, true worship is expressed. While such unbroken devotion is unattainable this side of eternity, the command communicates the need for purification in body and soul. Without comprehensive renewal, we can never and will never do all things for God's glory.

There is another reality in Paul's all-encompassing command. Given that the Spirit-renewed believer is called to this type of living, it means we possess the ability. We are given everything we need for a life of godliness (2 Pet 1:3). Though we are naturally prone to dishonor God, salvation renders glorifying him in all things possible—but not inevitable. The believer must act and do his or her part, a topic on which Paul offers further insight.

It seems that Paul understood the command to do everything to the glory of God might leave the believer's head spinning, so he offers some specifics. Instead of just saying to do everything for God's glory and leaving the believer to figure out the rest, he offers a reference point—the seemingly insignificant, everyday choices of eating and drinking. God deserves to be honored in even the most basic human requirements of life.

Logically, it follows that the command to honor God even in the consumption of foods and beverages means we can also dishonor him in these areas. Given our sinful nature, we are prone to dishonor him. This still applies particularly in an age where all types of foods, in gigantic quantities with untold additives, are readily available. And while Paul and other New Testament believers were not faced with the same processed, convenience, and fast-food choices we are today, that reality does not negate our same responsibility. If Paul was concerned about God's glory in these ordinary matters, it confirms that attention to how these choices impact our physical health must be a necessary consideration in the pursuit of holiness.

1 Corinthians 15

In 1 Corinthians 15, Paul clarifies the body's everlasting existence to establish its present and future worth, as many believers in Corinth were skeptical of their own bodily resurrection (15:12). Paul wrote the most content in each of his Corinthian letters on the necessity of resurrection—Christ's, and the surety that Christ-followers will be resurrected. He undoubtedly wanted the believers in Corinth to appreciate their promised, eternal embodiment because they were influenced by the gnostic culture around them. Paul, however, let the Corinthians know that it was incongruent to disbelieve their own resurrection while believing in a resurrected Christ. Jesus's physical, resurrected body confirms the gospel message and secures an eternal, embodied existence for believers. Affirming this message was essential, as so many other believers saw and testified to the tangible reality that Christ was bodily raised (15:6).

The belief in resurrection assures triumph over death and remains an emphatic tenet of Christianity (15:14, 55). Our faith withers without hope of a glorified body, but in Christ the firstfruits, our glorified body is guaranteed. (15:20). Resurrection will complete salvation, as all the benefits of salvation are not yet fully realized. In the present body, we possess the certainty of a future alteration to a glorious body like that of Christ's (Phil 3:21). Because the renewal experienced in salvation is a spiritual and physical one, Christians must not demean the body. It is a fundamental piece of our promised redemption and gospel proclamation. As this text holds important conclusions about the body, it receives further discussion in the next chapter.[19]

1 Timothy 4:7–8

> *Have nothing to do with irreverent, silly myths. Rather train yourself for godliness; for while bodily training is of some value, godliness is of value in every way, as it holds promise for the present life and also for the life to come.*

Paul communicates so much in 1 Tim 4:7–8, a text that seems to be a general statement on godly living. At

---

[19] Greer, "Utilization of a Theology of Human Embodiment," 30–34.

the outset, the inherent reality of embodiment is evident in Paul's statement for the value of both bodily training and training in godliness. Because there is some benefit to physical activity, the link between embodiment and holiness becomes clear. As body-and-soul beings, believers engage in spiritual and physical training.

This text is often taken one of two ways. The first reckons bodily training a waste of time, believing only godliness holds eternal import. The second understands that bodily training comes with value and engages in it, while properly prioritizing godliness. Whereas the first assumption misunderstands embodiment, the second gets it, recognizing the precedence of spiritual health and its connection to physical health. Consequently, two warnings can be distilled from this verse. One cautions against elevating physical fitness over godliness. This is idolatry. The other, "and far less acknowledged, admonition is against viewing the pursuit of physical health as an impediment to godliness. This is shortsighted."[20] It is exegetically unwarranted to wield this text as a means of dismissing exercise. Flatly,

---

[20] Lainey Greer, "Bodily Training Is of Some Value," *New Growth Press* (blog), July 28, 2022, https://blog.newgrowthpress.com/bodily-training-is-of-some-value/.

it is a strong, anti-body viewpoint that leads to such careless eisegesis.

Training for godliness, which is of highest value, does not imply the neglect of physical activity for a sole focus on spiritual matters. Furthermore, Paul's statement that bodily training is of some value seems inconsequential to his overall argument for pursuing godliness. This addition makes his comment noteworthy. To understand why Paul adds the comment in verse 8, we must consider its context. The exhortation to train oneself in godliness follows a warning against silly myths. Paul instructs Timothy to have nothing to do with them, but what exactly were these myths? Like every reading of Scripture, recognizing the context of these verses is critical.

Earlier in chapter 4, Paul discusses those who oppose marriage and prohibit the enjoyment of various foods—beliefs spawned by asceticism.[21] This idea denied the material to focus on the immaterial. Ascetics believed they could advance spiritually if they restrained themselves physically. From that viewpoint, they naturally misunderstood embodiment, thereby devaluing the tangible gifts of God's

[21] Asceticism is another anti-body philosophy to receive greater treatment in chapter 2.

good creation. Even more, Paul condemns the rejection of these gifts, instructing that they should be accepted with thanksgiving. As spiritual and physical beings, we, God's embodied image-bearers, are granted the ability to enjoy every part of his creative activity, which includes marriage, tasty food, and all other aspects of his physical creation we were designed to enjoy.

Having dealt with similar entanglements of asceticism in other churches, Paul condemns these anti-material arguments wherever they arise (1 Corinthians 7, 8, 10; Colossians 2). In his first letter to Timothy, he forbids the young pastor from having anything to do with ascetic notions that ultimately denigrate the body (see 1 Tim 4). Timothy's example to the believers in Ephesus was obviously critical, and Paul did not want him to be misled by these body-devaluing influences.

This setting renders Paul's mention of bodily training significant. In direct contradiction to the ascetics, Paul emphatically asserts that physical activity has some value. But why? Because believing the material body to be of lesser worth than the immaterial soul, ascetics would have had no use for bodily training. Undoubtedly, Timothy's focus should be godliness. At the same time, he ought not be swayed by a sanctimonious spirituality that could breed an anti-body approach to life. Believers today cannot make the same mistake made by the ascetics Timothy was to avoid. Whether from ignorance or negligence, for the church to deride the body as evil or insignificant is a denial of God's Word.

From this limited analysis of Scripture, particularly Genesis 1–2 and pertinent Pauline texts, it is evident that the Christian faith concerns every area of life. As we will give an account for everything done in the body (2 Cor 5:10), what Christians do or fail to do in our present, embodied state matters.

2

An Anthropological Argument for the Body

"I appeal to you therefore, brothers, by the mercies of God, to present your bodies as a living sacrifice, holy and acceptable to God, which is your spiritual worship" (Rom 12:1). An embodied understanding of holiness associates bodily submission with spiritual worship. This chapter presents the necessity of embodiment for human constitution. After brief descriptions of monistic and dualistic anthropologies, the most biblical, logical understanding of humanity will be given. Humans as a holistic dualism is a view that accounts for the value of both body and soul while also recognizing the need for an intermediate state between death and resurrection. For that reason, the heart of this chapter will argue for humans as a holistic dualism, a helpful rendering from John Cooper that corrects erroneous views of embodiment and the anti-body sentiments they spawn.[1] This chapter's content holds great significance for the one that follows. If we view the body through a filter that devalues the material, then we will misunderstand the body's role in holy living.

Embodiment

Embodiment is the natural form of all human beings who are both immaterial soul and material body. Humans are spiritually fitted for a relationship with the Creator and physically fitted to enjoy the world he created. In emphasizing the soul and spiritual matters, though necessary to our

---

[1] Joshua Farris estimates that

> John Cooper's work is the most thorough biblical defense of dualism (e.g., substance dualism, Thomist dualism) in the literature to date. . . . By carefully working through Old Testament, intertestamental, New Testament, and ancient writings, Cooper shows quite plainly that the metaphysical implication of the biblical data is dualism, not monism.

Joshua R. Farris, *An Introduction to Theological Anthropology: Humans, Both Creaturely and Divine* (Baker Academic, 2020), 288.

personhood, Christians have tended to overlook the body, a reality this chapter explains. The reality of corporeality unites all people all over the world for all of time. Human existence and experience depend on it. It is through the body that we see, hear, feel, taste, smell, and touch. Apart from these physical senses, we lack the capacity to behold a creation that points to our Creator. So, as beings purposefully designed with spiritual and physical abilities, Christians should appreciate the body alongside the soul. Embodiment is essential. While we are disembodied for a time in the intermediate state, which will be further explained in this chapter, embodied reality is God's intent, from creation to re-creation.[2]

Embodiment is best understood as part of a theology of the body because Scripture attests to both immaterial and material existence. Embodied reality also recognizes the psychosomatic connection and interaction between mind and body that God designed for human flourishing. This

---

[2] Gregg R. Allison states, "The intermediate state is the condition of people between their physical death and the return of Jesus Christ (with the accompanying event of bodily resurrection). Importantly, the state of disembodiment is abnormal for human beings created as embodied image bearers of God." Gregg R. Allison, *Embodied: Living as Whole People in a Fractured World* (Baker, 2021), 248.

interconnection results in the influence of one on the other. Mind impacts body, just as the body effects the mind. This psychosomatic connection tied to embodiment shows the necessity of immaterial and material functioning, making both significant in daily life.[3] This chapter's reflection on various biblical terms will demonstrate that significance.

Furthermore, there is no biblical basis for prizing soul above body, as each aspect relies on the other.[4] A physical body and spiritual soul serve as equal prerequisites for being human, and the embodied person is God's distinctive, marvelous creation. Both intentional design and wondrous purpose lie behind the functions of soul and body. It is in our bodies that God places us in the exact time and space he sovereignly chooses, so that we will come to

---

[3] Parenthetically, when speaking of the soul and spiritual capacities, I mean to encompass thoughts of the mind and feelings of the heart as evidence of immaterial existence.

[4] Contradicting this tendency, Vernon Elmore explains, "It is alien to the Bible to think of the body as an inferior product and as an embarrassment to the soul since the body is in the image of God as well as the rest of his being. The body should be treated with dignity and not considered the seat of evil and to be looked upon with contempt." Vernon Elmore, *Man as God's Creation: Layman's Library of Christian Doctrine* (Broadman, 1986), 35. Because the body matters for Christian living, we must agree with this fundamental teaching on its value alongside the soul.

know him, relating to him through our souls. Embodied existence is meant to drive us back to him as his holistically dependent offspring (Acts 17:26–28).

Still, the body may be unappreciated due to its normality and may be forgotten about until illness, injury, or unwanted effects of aging occur.[5] Worse, it is abused through

---

[5] McBride agrees. "For those of us who are able-bodied," she says, "it may have been possible for a time for us to remain unconscious of our embodiment or repress it altogether, leading to a dissociated self within the body; it is the sensations of pain or dis-ease which most often require a person to notice their body in a way that they may not have before." Hillary L. McBride, "Embodiment and Body Image," in *Embodiment and Eating Disorders: Theory, Research, Prevention, and Treatment*, ed. Hillary L. McBride and Janelle L. Kwee (Routledge, 2019), 11. Detailing his "bodily experience of diminishment," Johnson is quite candid about physical changes have caused a new awareness of his body:

> The decade of my sixties, especially the last half, was the most revealing in terms of physical change. All at once, it seems, the warranty elapses, and everything starts to fall apart. It is, of course, not "all at once," but just another stage in a long process. But now I am alert to my weaknesses more than I am to my strengths. . . . My body now seems to me less a reliable friend than an unpredictable and sometimes resentful companion. My eyes are worse, my hearing is bad . . . , and arthritis stabs me with pain. . . . I have hypertension. My weight

starvation and overexercise, as in my case, when it fails to live up to unattainable expectations, or is intentionally destroyed by acts of self-harm.[6] Surely, God wants more for the body that he created, indwells, and will resurrect.

Insufficient knowledge of a theology of the body and embodied reality continues today in various forms, with Gnosticism being the common denominator.[7] The solution is a proper theological understanding of the body and

---

> insists on staying. My hair is white and thinning. . . . My lower back is in very bad shape. I now need to walk an hour every day, and faithfully do back exercises, simply to remain mobile. I don't even think about picking up the ball and throwing it; the thought of the consequent pain in my shoulder is sufficient to prevent any such fantasy. Indeed I cannot really remember my muscular and athletic body. . . . My aging process is absolutely normal. But I still don't like it.

Luke Timothy Johnson, *The Revelatory Body: Theology as Inductive Art* (Eerdmans, 2015), 210–11.

[6] Cutting and burning are the most common self-harming behaviors. Research shows that one in four girls and one in ten boys have participated in intentional self-harm. Lindsay Kite and Lexie Kite, *More Than a Body: Your Body Is an Instrument Not an Ornament* (Houghton Mifflin Harcourt, 2020), 20.

[7] Gnosticism, to be addressed in this chapter, perpetuates today with concerning implications for the body. According to Allison, "Neo-Gnosticism . . . continues to infect the church,

a robust recognition of embodiment. For a faith that rests on the belief that God became man, Christians cannot afford to pit the spiritual against the physical, as do those who reject the body's goodness.

Naturally, anthropology connects to embodiment, and is an additional weak point in evangelicalism, likely because Scripture does not present a detailed anthropology.[8] For Christians, anthropological discussion should encompass the way humans are formed such that they live in a physical world and yet can commune with a spiritual being. Without a proper anthropology and right understanding of embodiment, we lose the Creator-creature distinction. We negate not only our created design but the purpose we were created for, the end our lives are designed to pursue.

Sorting out these issues involving embodiment and anthropology requires discussing two philosophical positions on the nature of humankind: monism and dualism. Monism determines that humans are only one part (*either* the material part *or* the immaterial part), while dualism views human nature in two parts (the material body and

---

leading to disregard for, distancing oneself from, or disparagement of the body." Allison, *Embodied*, 28.

[8] Anthony Hoekema, *Created in God's Image* (1986; repr., Eerdmans, 1994), 204.

the immaterial soul).[9] While these sections are not intended to be thorough treatments of either position, an overview of each will suffice for the determination of a clear, biblical understanding of the body.[10]

Monism

Monism posits that there are no distinguishing aspects of human composition. While there are several forms of monism, materialism will be the focus here. Materialists propose that humans are material beings without any immaterial aspect.[11] Many rely on scientific evidence, reasoning that the brain alone animates humans, rendering the soul's influence unnecessary.[12] So, humans are purely

---

[9] Warren S. Brown and Brad D. Strawn, *The Physical Nature of Christian Life: Neuroscience, Psychology, and the Church* (Cambridge University Press, 2012), 5.

[10] Greer, "The Utilization of a Theology of Human Embodiment to Address Body Image," 40–43.

[11] Farris, *Introduction to Theological Anthropology*, 2.

[12] Hans Madueme, "From Sin to the Soul," in *The Christian Doctrine of Humanity: Explorations in Constructive Dogmatics*, ed. Oliver D. Crisp and Fred Sanders (Zondervan, 2018), 71; see also Robert Pyne, *Humanity and Sin: Creation, Fall, and Redemption of Humanity* (Thomas Nelson, 1999), 77.

material beings, and any emotional, spiritual, or mental happenings are attributed to biological processes.[13] However, materialism reduces the nature of humans to a point that is antithetical to Scripture, going against God's formation of the first humans from dust and breath (Gen 2:7). The materialist dismisses such texts, supposing they are imported with unintended meaning.[14]

---

[13] See Brandon Rickabaugh and J. P. Moreland, *The Substance of Consciousness: Comprehensive Defense of Contemporary Substance Dualism* (Wiley Blackwell, 2023).

[14] Brown and Strawn, *Physical Nature*, 17. Furthermore, Brown and Strawn hold that

> what is inside us that accounts for our distinctiveness as humankind is not an immaterial thing, such as a soul, that is separate from our bodies and needs a particular form of spiritual care and nurture. Rather, inside us are myriad complex physical functions and processes, shaped both by our physical development and by our history of personal experiences. These functions and processes contribute bits and pieces to who we are as rational, social, moral, and religious whole-physical persons capable of interacting with the physical, social, and spiritual world within which we are embedded.

Brown and Strawn, *Physical Nature*, 47.

Unsurprisingly, this belief is a basis for denying God and the creation of humans in the *imago Dei*. This reality means that many materialists are atheists who see the soul and spiritual capacity as antiquated beliefs, though some materialists claim faith in Christ.[15] The trouble is materialism cannot support a biblical eschatology without stretching the limits of its beliefs. Materialism asserts that one's mind is also understood as the brain; therefore, if the brain dies, the mind dies. If true, then the person ceases to exist at death, which is a complete rejection of the Scriptures promising life after death.[16] Relatedly, materialism must also deny the reality of the intermediate state, having no reason to believe in existence beyond physical death.

Still, in hopes of retaining belief in the resurrection, Christian materialists generally adopt a view of immediate resurrection or extinction re-creation.[17] These after-death

---

[15] See Warren S. Brown, Nancey Murphy, and H. Newton Maloney, eds., *Whatever Happened to the Soul? Scientific and Theological Portraits of Human Nature*, Theology and the Sciences (Fortress, 1998); Kevin Corcoran, *Rethinking Human Nature: A Christian Materialist Alternative to the Soul* (Baker Academic, 2006); and Joel B. Green, *Body, Soul, and Human Life: The Nature of Humanity in the Bible* (Baker Academic, 2008).

[16] Pyne, *Humanity and Sin*, 80.

[17] Farris, *Introduction to Theological Anthropology*, 238.

views are important to include for determining what kind of future existence God promises, which aids in our examination of embodiment.

Immediate Resurrection and Extinction Re-Creation

The immediate resurrection position holds that humans are instantly resurrected upon death.[18] In this understanding, proponents avoid the problem of soul and body coming apart, though how exactly this happens is up for debate.[19] Some believe that Christians enter a new dimension involving a new conception of time.[20] Others spiritualize the resurrection of believers at Christ's return to avoid the dualistic composition that death and eternal existence requires.[21] So, proponents of immediate resurrection have no need for an interluding state of disembodied existence.

---

[18] Farris, 2.

[19] Pyne, *Humanity and Sin*, 80.

[20] See James T. Turner Jr., *On the Resurrection of the Dead: A New Metaphysics of Afterlife for Christian Thought* (Routledge, 2018).

[21] For more on immediate resurrection, see Murray J. Harris, *From Grave to Glory: Resurrection in the New Testament* (Zondervan, 1990), 185–230.

Supporters of extinction re-creation hold that material beings cease to exist upon death, and in essence wait on God to supply a re-created, revived, resurrected being.[22] This view seems even more extreme than immediate resurrection, as its supporters go to great lengths to circumvent the soul's continued existence after death. Extinction re-creation orders the human experience from existence, to complete nonexistence, and to re-existence again, which also counters an intermediate state.

Other Postmortem Beliefs

Were humans a dual substance then none of these monistic arguments for what happens after death would hold. However, for monists to maintain that humans are purely material, they must explicitly deny the intermediate state and work around texts that communicate any sort of existence after death.

---

[22] Farris, *Introduction to Theological Anthropology*, 239. Nancey Murphy's view on non-reductive physicalism is one such position that denies an intermediate state and supports resurrection as re-creation. Nancey Murphy, "Human Nature: Historical, Scientific, and Religious Issues," in Brown, Murphy, and Maloney, *Whatever Happened to the Soul?*, 25.

Soul Sleep. Soul sleep holds that, after death, people continue to exist in God's mind or consciousness.[23] In this view, following death, believers are thought to remain unconscious, awaiting Christ's return. Then, at resurrection, they return to consciousness.[24] Adherents to this view base it on biblical passages that mention believers who have died as being asleep. However, a plain reading of the text makes clear the writers are simply communicating death is not permanent (e.g., Jer 51:39; Acts 7:60; 1 Cor 15:18).[25] Such statements were meant to encourage living believers (1 Thess 4:15–18). This view, which is akin to cessation, must be discounted, as Scripture describes the believer as enjoying immediate consciousness with God at death (Luke 23:43, Phil 1:23; Rev 6:9–11).[26]

---

[23] Farris, *Introduction to Theological Anthropology*, 239.

[24] Wayne Grudem, *Systematic Theology: An Introduction to Biblical Doctrine*, 2nd ed. (Zondervan, 2020), 1008. Stephen T. Davis questions the viability of this belief, implying the incoherence of a bodiless soul that engages in sleep, a bodily activity. Stephen T. Davis, *After We Die: Theology, Philosophy, and the Question of Life After Death* (Baylor University Press, 2015), 61.

[25] Grudem, *Systematic Theology*, 1009.

[26] Grudem, 1010.

Cessation. Cessation views life with finality, a natural conclusion from the monist belief that existence ends in permanent death. In death, the soul ceases to exist, and the body lies in decay. Secularization, modernism, and scientific advances have spurred on this belief, considering Christian teaching on life after death antiquated and simplistic.[27] Believers who hold to cessation found their claims on texts such as Gen 3:19 and Eccl 3:19–20 as evidence that human existence ceases upon death.[28] Like soul sleep, this view contradicts the promise of life after death that Christ's resurrection secures (1 Cor 15:12–20).

Annihilationism. Annihilationists reckon that God eventually terminates those who die in their sins to keep them from suffering eternal punishment in hell, which links to the monist belief that death ends existence. Supporters of

---

[27] Notions like these are seen throughout the *Humanist Manifestos I* (1933), *II* (1973), *III* (2003). These manifestos are available to view on the website of the American Humanist Association at https://americanhumanist.org/what-is-humanism/manifesto1/; https://americanhumanist.org/what-is-humanism/manifesto2/; and https://americanhumanist.org/what-is-humanism/manifesto3/.

[28] Farris, *Introduction to Theological Anthropology*, 235; James R. Beck and Bruce A. Demarest, *The Human Person in Theology and Psychology: A Biblical Anthropology for the Twenty-First Century* (Kregel, 2005), 47–48.

annihilation reject hell as an eternal judgment where God pours out his wrath against those who lived in rebellion and denial of him.[29] Holding this belief as inconsistent with a loving God, they claim he will simply annihilate unbelievers to spare them from his wrath. Given there are texts that address an eternal torment without mentioning termination, annihilationism is not only inconsistent with Scripture but also Christ's own words about the coming judgment unbelievers face (Matt 8:12; 25:30; 2 Thess 1:9; Jude 6).[30]

In sum, this short overview shows that a monist anthropology cannot be supported by Scripture and discounts the goodness of God's design for embodied beings made to embody holiness in soul and body.

Dualism

Not only do the tenets of monism run counter to Scripture, but they also contradict the evidence of an embodied

---

[29] Some proponents prefer the terminology of conditional immortality. See Edward W. Fudge, *Hell: A Final Word* (Leafwood, 2012); or John R. W. Stott, "The Gospel for the World: Response," in *Evangelical Essentials: A Liberal-Evangelical Dialogue*, ed. David L. Edwards (InterVarsity Press, 1988).

[30] Greer, "Utilization of a Theology," 44–51.

humanity and biblical depictions of an afterlife. Instead, deducing an accurate biblical anthropology leads to dualism, which recognizes the constitution of humans as body-and-soul beings alongside promises of future resurrection and eternal existence. Dualists generally hold to a two-part ontological makeup of humanity: body and soul, material and immaterial, physical and spiritual.[31] This dual construction is evident even from a brief scan of Scripture that shows God speaking to, using, guiding, and providing for a people who have both spiritual and physical capacities, being equally in need of spiritual and physical renewal owing to the embodied effects of sin.[32]

---

[31] This view likely originated from Tertullian, who upheld the necessity of Christ's bodily substance largely in response to the heretic Marcion. Gregg R. Allison, *Historical Theology: An Introduction to Christian Doctrine* (Zondervan Academic, 2011), 324. Tertullian's work *On the Flesh of Christ* is an important example of Christians who strongly affirmed the body's value in the face of those who devalued it. Tertullian, *On the Flesh of Christ*, in *The Christological Controversy*, ed. and trans. Richard A. Norris Jr., Sources of Early Christian Thought (Fortress, 1980).

[32] On affirming a dualist anthropology, Madueme grounds his argument in hamartiology, which coheres with the reality of sin more than a materialist view. He comments, "The most plausible significance of the biblical language is that the volitional,

Historically, substance dualism has been the dominant view of the church, understanding the human as a rational soul and physical body.[33] Like monism, there are numerous forms of dualism; however, two stand out as most relevant to this work. The first is axiological dualism, which believes in a two-part construction but elevates soul over body and spiritual matters over physical ones. The second is anthropological dualism, which also holds to a two-part makeup but treats soul and body equally, recognizing the value in spiritual and physical realities. The difference is critical. Anthropological dualism values the body, while axiological dualism devalues it. Therefore, they should not be conflated. Scripture presents a form of anthropological dualism, whereas axiological dualism plagues the church, with particularly devastating effects on how Christians

---

moral core of humanity is not exhausted by the physical. . . . Human sinfulness is a problem that tracks deeper than our physical bodies. This problem inheres in our very souls. . . . Embodiment gives our sins a 'bodily' character." Madueme, "From Sin to the Soul," 84–85.

[33] Farris, *Introduction to Theological Anthropology*, 2. Seeing humans as a complexity with immaterial and material parts, historically the church "wrestled with views that disparage the body and treat it as being inherently evil." Allison, *Historical Theology*, 321.

treat their own bodies and address cultural issues that involve the body.

Axiological Dualism

Axiological dualism ascribes a significance to the soul that far outweighs any importance of the body. The soul is deemed as having inherent worth; the body is seen as the source of sin.[34] Most axiological dualists liken the distinction to good versus evil; so, the link between immaterial and material is contentious. The soul is elevated and the body denigrated.[35] Often, this viewpoint assumes a great disparity between the two parts that will not be alleviated until the soul is set free from the body in death.[36]

---

[34] Throughout this chapter, I rely on Cooper's definition of axiological dualism in John W. Cooper, *Body, Soul, and Life Everlasting: Biblical Anthropology and the Monism-Dualism Debate* (Eerdmans, 2000), 185.

[35] Cooper, *Body, Soul, and Life Everlasting*, 185.

[36] Lactantius's view of the body demonstrates this thinking: "But when a separation shall have been made between the body and the soul [at death], then evil will be disunited from good; and as the body perishes and the soul remains, so evil will perish and good be permanent. Then man, having received the

This hierarchical distinction between soul and body likely originates from two main factors. First, the early church spread the gospel message to a world largely dominated by Hellenistic culture. Second, the predominant language for New Testament writers and philosophical leaders was Greek, making the comingling of Christian beliefs and Hellenistic ideologies unavoidable. Many Greek philosophers held the mind and mental pursuits superior to all else. So, debasement of the body and its more animalistic tendencies in their thinking was inevitable.[37] With the mind viewed as the connection to spirituality, it is clear

---

garment of immortality, will be wise and free from evil, as God is." Lactanius, *The Divine Institutes* 7.5, in *ANF* 7:202.

[37] Noting this inevitability, Deborah Beth Creamer writes:

> The Judeo-Christian tradition(s) developed in a world that already had abundant assumptions and interpretations of the body. Plato contributed much of what was further developed by Descartes, the separation of form and matter, body and soul, . . . that set up inescapable groundwork for Christian interpretations of embodiment and difference.

Deborah Beth Creamer, *Disability and Christian Theology: Embodied Limits and Constructive Possibilities* (Oxford University Press, 2009), 41.

how these thoughts blended in with focus on the divine for believers. In this way, anti-body anthropologies assimilated into Christianity.[38] Still, some believers recognized this concerning linkage of non-Christian anthropology with Christian belief and its detrimental effects that spawned erroneous theologies of the body. Just as they combated this thinking in the past, the task continues today.

To correct an axiological dualism in Christian practice, the church would do well to reconsider human composition. Therefore, the remainder of the chapter will examine Platonism and Gnosticism, which led to the practice of asceticism. Following an overview of each, these anti-body anthropologies will be challenged with an explanation of humans as a holistic dualism.

Platonism. The Greek philosopher Plato (428–348 BC) believed that a person's true nature was located in the intellect.[39] Seeing the material as an obstacle to the immaterial part of humanity, he taught that the soul's freedom and salvation were not achieved until death. In physical death, the true, spiritual aspect continues. In this, the

---

[38] Charles Sherlock, *The Doctrine of Humanity*, Contours of Christian Theology (IVP Academic, 1997), 77.

[39] Plato, *The Timaeus*, 90C.

soul is proven divine, unlike the body.[40] Additionally, Plato believed that people are characterized by rational and irrational aspects. The rational side found in the mind controls irrational appetites found in the body. So, to Plato, the body hinders the soul. Therefore, in his reckoning, spiritual virtue comes with physical denial.[41]

The influence of Platonic thought on the church is often called Christian Platonism. Notwithstanding a strong critique of Gnosticism that is similarly anti-body, Christian Platonism became prevalent because several church fathers endorsed aspects of it.[42] This surprising approval arose because many early Christians were Platonists before coming to faith in Christ. Thinking Plato's views on human nature were correct, new converts maintained their former anthropological beliefs. Naturally, the tendencies of axiological dualism continued and were incorporated into the works of church fathers like Justin Martyr, Cyprian, and Augustine.[43] As Cooper notes, such works "became almost canonical in the history of Christian doctrine,

---

[40] Plato, *Phaedo*; Hoekema, *Created in God's Image*, 2.

[41] Hoekema, *Created in God's Image*, 41.

[42] Cooper, *Body, Soul, and Life Everlasting*, 185.

[43] Cooper, 25.

systematically read the Greek mind into the Scriptures and elaborated it as theological orthodoxy," a grave error that was unfortunately maintained for years to come.[44]

Augustine held that the person is located in the superior soul, which enlivens the inferior body.[45] He shifted Plato's tripartite view to combine soul and spirit, which contrasted with the body. Though he understood humans as a material and immaterial unity, Augustine still elevated soul above body.[46] That said, he did diverge from Plato in a couple of areas. First, he believed in the creation of souls over their eternal existence. Second, Augustine did not view the body as evil, despite his beliefs that elevated the soul as superior.[47] Most significantly, he taught that

---

[44] Cooper, 26.

[45] Calvin could also be included. Farris sees a "collection of views in the Plato-Augustine-Calvin-Descartes tradition, where there is a distinction between person and body, wherein the person is strictly identical to the soul, or the soul is the core of the person, and the body is contingent." Farris, *Introduction to Theological Anthropology*, 76.

[46] Augustine of Hippo, *On Faith and the Creed* 10.23 (*NPNF*[1] 3:331); *On the Soul and Its Origin* 4.3 (*NPNF*[1] 5:355); Beck and Demarest, *Human Person in Theology*, 125.

[47] Augustine, *Tractates on the Gospel of John* 47.11 (*NPNF*[1] 7:264).

the soul alone bears God's image, a view that can spawn devastating consequences for the body. Believing the body a distraction to the soul, his anthropological conceptions furthered the church's misperceptions of the body.[48]

Trichotomy. Trichotomy, another take on humanity's constitution, has its roots in Platonism.[49] This view lies within dualism because trichotomists begin with the belief that the material and immaterial separate at death.[50] From there, they diverge from dualists on the number of aspects that make up humanity, sectioning them into three parts—body, spirit, and soul/mind—leaving a material part and two immaterial parts. The spirit is held up as the real self, which relates to God and must remain separate from the body. Thus, the soul connects the two disparate parts, spirit and body, functioning as mediator between immaterial and material.[51]

Trichotomists locate their arguments primarily in 1 Thess 5:23 and Heb 4:12. In 1 Thess 5:23, Paul specifies

---

[48] Augustine, *Literal Meaning of Genesis* 1.15.29, cited in Cooper, *Body, Soul, and Life Everlasting*, 10.

[49] Cooper, *Body, Soul, and Life Everlasting*, 9. See also Beck and Demarest, *Human Person in Theology*, 127.

[50] Pyne, *Humanity and Sin*, 102.

[51] Cooper, *Body, Soul, and Life Everlasting*, 9.

the body, soul, and spirit, which is taken to be an obvious description of humanity's tripartite nature. They also rely on a phrase in Heb 4:12 that seems to indicate that soul and spirit are divisible substances. Passages like Job 7:11 and Luke 1:46–47 are taken as testifying to a soul distinct from spirit.[52] Finally, another verse used as evidence for three parts in humanity is 1 Cor 14:14. Here Paul laments that his spirit prays while his mind remains unfruitful. To trichotomists, these verses reveal a separation between the activities of the spirit versus the soul. In turn, they attribute thinking to the soul rather than the spirit.[53]

Those who disagree with trichotomy offer simple explanations for these tripartite-labeled verses. Various Scriptures pile up similar words to amplify descriptions. Paul uses three terms in 1 Thess 5:23 to emphasize the need for purity in the last days.[54] Additionally, understanding the context of Heb 4:12 negates a trichotomist view. If the author was teaching a distinction between soul and spirit, then it logically follows that joints and marrow should be considered similarly distinct. Instead, the focus

---

52 Pyne, *Humanity and Sin*, 103.

53 Grudem, *Systematic Theology*, 606.

54 Sherlock, *Doctrine of Humanity*, 218.

is on Scripture's divine power, not divisions in human constitution. The tripartite view fails to provide a persuasive, biblical argument for the human composition.[55]

While trichotomists unduly divide human persons, gnostics give disproportionate worth to soul over body, classifying their anthropological understanding as an axiological dualism.

Gnosticism. With its roots in Platonism, Gnosticism became prominent in the second century AD, though Christians combated early forms in the New Testament. A central teaching of this philosophy held the material as evil and the immaterial as good, thereby denigrating and devaluing bodily existence.[56] Because they associated creation with the fall, gnostics viewed God as totally set apart from the physical world, having nothing to do with it. This belief inevitably resulted in disdain for the material world.[57] Corruption was tied to the body, and gnostics saw themselves as superior to anything that involved

---

[55] As trichotomy remains unconvincing, the natural conclusion would be to affirm a dichotomy in human constitution.

[56] Allison, *Embodied*, 27.

[57] Michael A. G. Haykin, "This Anthropological Moment," *Eikon: A Journal for Biblical Anthropology* 1, no. 2 (2019): 6.

physicality. This thinking had a twofold result. First, the goodness of the body and created things were denied. Second, a higher, spiritual knowledge was pursued, one unsurprisingly disconnected from the body. They felt this hidden knowledge was integral to a pious, devout lifestyle, deeming the body a hindrance and physical resurrection undesirable. For these reasons, this conception of human constitution qualifies Gnosticism as an axiological view.

Gnostics also surmised that there were numerous evil gods, ranking them from the most to least powerful. Creation was viewed as the product of a lesser, evil god, while more powerful gods were thought to be uninvolved in material things. Such beliefs are extreme contrasts to the immanent yet transcendent Creator God of the Bible. Gnostics also viewed death as severing the soul from the burdensome body. Thus, salvation meant escaping matter, whereas in Christianity, salvation promises the restoration of matter.[58]

Unsurprisingly, gnostics deny that the Son of God would lower himself to assume a physical, human body. By

---

[58] Lactantius, *The Divine Institutes* 4.25 (*ANF* 7:127); *Letter to Diognetus* 6 (*ANF* 1:27); Nancy R. Pearcey, *Love Thy Body: Answering Hard Questions About Life and Sexuality* (Baker Books, 2018), 36–38; Allison, *Embodied*, 27.

rejecting the incarnation, the cross and everything Christ's atonement achieved is lost, which is why accounts of his crucifixion are not found in the Gnostic Gospels.[59] When created material is seen as evil and the source of wickedness, the effect is clear: the notion of God becoming man is inconceivable. The anthropological assumptions in Gnosticism contradicted central Christian doctrines like creation, the incarnation, the hypostatic union, and resurrection.[60] Faithful Christ followers have set out to disparage this philosophy ever since.

In his first epistle, John went after a form of Gnosticism that infected the early church. He begins his first epistle by declaring the validity of the embodied Christ. The very reality that John bodily saw and touched Jesus's body verifies his testimony that eternal life is found in Christ alone (1 John 1:1). Later, in chapter 4, to combat false teaching, John reports that the test for faithful Christian believers is whether they affirm that Christ came in the flesh (1 John 4:2). Once again, Christ's physical, bodily resurrection becomes the proof of saving

---

[59] Fleming Rutledge, *The Crucifixion: Understanding the Death of Jesus* (Eerdmans, 2015), 50.

[60] Allison, *Embodied*, 27.

belief. John is unwavering: To deny the fleshly existence of Christ is to deny the gospel. Finally, he writes in 5:8 that the Spirit, water, and blood validate that the Son of God came in the flesh. The divine testimony of the Spirit and Christ's broken body on the cross—the literal elements that prove his physical life—verify his person and work. As Christ's body is consequential to the gospel, so the believer's body is critical in demonstrating the gospel's transforming power.

Or consider Irenaeus, who arose as an ardent defender of Christianity against the gnostic threat in his *Against Heresies*. He also understood the importance of Christ's body to the faith and even recognized the body's integral role in image bearing. Against proponents of Gnosticism, he claimed that there would be no image apart from the body.[61] Just as Christ's death and resurrection ensures the redemption of soul and body, together with the soul the body is esteemed as bearing the *imago Dei*.

Gnosticism spawned a variety of other heretical views, such as Docetism, Arianism, Apollinarianism, and Nestorianism, all of which distorted Christ's incarnation

---

[61] Irenaeus of Lyon, *Against Heresies* 4, preface, para. 4 (*ANF* 1:462–63).

and hypostatic union. Pivotal councils in the early church pushed back on these views to define Christ's deity (Nicaea I, Constantinople I) and Christ's humanity (Ephesus, Chalcedon, Constantinople II, Nicaea II, and Constantinople III). These important efforts should continue to inform the church's Christology, as misunderstandings of Christ's humanity continue today.[62]

---

[62] Kelly M. Kapic understands the lingering Christological issues that impact current Christian anthropology. He writes:

> One can argue that over the past 150 years evangelicals in the West have spent a great deal more of their energy defending the deity of Jesus the Messiah than examining the equally important confession of his full human nature. If you ask many Christians today, "Do you believe that Jesus was really a human?" they normally nod their heads without hesitation: but experience makes me wonder if we understand that doctrine and its implications. . . . I believe that many evangelicals, for example, have not fully embraced or worked out the implications of believing that their Savior, the Son of God, is also the son of Mary.

Kelly M. Kapic, *You're Only Human: How Your Limits Reflect God's Design and Why That's Good News* (Brazos, 2022), 42. Similar to Kapic's experience, I have also endured direct criticism of my work in a theology of the body, which validates Kapic's Christological concerns.

Because Gnosticism flourished in a setting where material things were maligned, it should come as no surprise that a similar contempt of the body remains. This is why the church must dismantle the deleterious effects of Gnosticism and all its lingering forms. After all, if believers fail to recognize the significance of embodiment, then how can they properly value the body and assent to its vital role in holy living?

Just as the gnostic conception of spirituality rejected the material realm, ascetics reflect a similar denunciation of physicality, qualifying it as an anti-body anthropology.

Asceticism. Monasticism arose out of the early church, expanded in the medieval period, and is closely associated with asceticism.[63] The ascetic's way of living often focused on bridling the body to advance the soul. Such ascetic practices naturally flow from an axiological dualism, maligning material realities to focus on immaterial ones.[64] Highly influenced by Platonic thought, ascetics believed that pursuing holiness meant denying the body

[63] For more on asceticism, consider Ranald Macaulay and Jerram Barrs, *Being Human: The Nature of Spiritual Experience* (IVP Academic, 1998).

[64] Cooper, *Body, Soul, and Life Everlasting*, 185. See also Pearcey, *Love Thy Body*, 41; Allison, *Embodied*, 154.

any form of pleasure, such as enjoying tasty food or physical intimacy, wearing decent clothing, and even sleeping in a comfortable bed.[65]

Consequently, believers perceived the material body as an undesirable hindrance to spiritual pursuits. Efforts in sanctification required engaging the soul and restraining the body. Unsurprisingly, ascetics sought displacement from the world and its physical entailments by whatever means necessary. This type of devotion was deemed more spiritual than living a regular life where bodily pleasures were enjoyed. An anti-body anthropology drove this lifestyle that related the soul with godliness and the body with folly, making it another instance of axiological dualism.

In the face of asceticism, Paul fervently defends the value of bodily existence. As evidenced in chapter 1, he contradicts those who argued for the avoidance of marriage and certain foods because they both brought bodily pleasure. Paul wanted Timothy, a key young church leader,

---

[65] On the influence of asceticism in the Middle Ages, Allison remarks that "the church's theology and practice suffered dramatically because of it." Allison, *Historical Theology*, 328. As we will see in the later, practical chapters, this problem continues. The church's physical condition suffers from mistaken views of the body.

to be assured the body was part of God's good creation, even as he stressed pursuing godliness (1 Tim 4:7–8).

In Colossae, believers were in danger of ascetic thinking. Paul again went out of his way to reference the body in a context under the influence of an errant theology of the body. First, referring to the church as Christ's body of whom he is head (Col 1:18), Paul proclaimed their reconciliation by Christ's death (1:22). Interestingly, while the mention of Christ's death would have sufficed for Paul's point, he tacks on a unique phrase: fleshly body. Through Christ's body of flesh, a clear redundancy, the Colossians are made right with God. Arguably, Paul's emphasis on the body acts as a means of proving to the Colossians that Christ's body, and their own bodies, mattered.[66]

But Paul goes on. Like John in the face of gnostic teaching, Paul leaves no room for doubt that the Son of God became incarnate, stating that the fullness of deity took on a bodily presence (2:9). Against those insisting on asceticism, Paul admonishes the Colossian body of Christ to hold fast to the head. Here again Paul goes into unnecessarily specific

[66] Kilner understands these ascetic notions viewed holy living as separate from the body, which "unbiblically demeans" it. John F. Kilner, *Dignity and Destiny: Humanity in the Image of God* (Eerdmans, 2015), 195.

details about the body, particularly its physical makeup, to emphasize the believer's union with Christ (2:19). Furthermore, some in Colossae engaged in the harsh treatment of the body taught by the ascetics—restraining the body to advance the soul. But Paul condemns measures that push man-made legalism against the body and its physical senses. Citing this façade of piety as useless against the sinful nature, he contends that this so-called wisdom possesses no value in combating sin (Col 2:21–23). Chiefly, Paul's arguments against the asceticism in Colossae not only stand against self-imposed religious standards but also protect the body's importance. Christians today should take note, as many subconsciously operate with an ascetic mindset regarding the body, disconnecting spirituality from physicality.[67]

It is true that various New Testament authors speak against bodily sins, but it is inappropriate to use these instances as fodder for labeling the body the singular source of corruption. As Paul demonstrates in Eph 2:2, the passions of our sinful nature (*sarx*) characterize desires

---

[67] Anecdotally, many times after I speak on these topics, people share how they have unknowingly held these thoughts about the body and holy living. It is likely that many Christians are unaware that they operate with such a misunderstood theology of the body.

of both body and mind. In 1 Thessalonians, rather than harshly treating the body over sexual immorality as an ascetic would, Paul commands bodily holiness. Believers fight against physical sins by striving with the Spirit to control the body in ways that look different from the conduct of unbelievers (1 Thess 4:3–4). Sexual sin will not be defeated by controlling the body alone; rather, altering the mind and heart, all of which is empowered by the Spirit, orients the embodied believer toward holy endeavors.

Per Bavinck, if the body alone bears the blame for sin, then salvation could be manufactured via asceticism.[68] But as the case for this lifestyle cannot be made from Scripture, it is only those who import Greek philosophies into a biblical anthropology who commend it. The overlap of these anti-body, axiological beliefs—Platonism, Gnosticism, and asceticism—with Christianity requires us to be honest with ourselves, paying careful attention even to subconscious views of the body. As the church's

---

[68] Herman Bavinck, *Reformed Ethics*, vol. 1, *Created, Fallen, and Converted Humanity*, ed. and trans. John Bolt (Baker Academic, 2019), 91. On unbiblical conceptions of the body, Bavinck continues, "The human ability to subject the body and make it subservient to the soul can still be seen in the asceticism of the Stoics and monastics." Bavinck, 152.

spiritual mission lies in a physical world, the labors of an embodied soul are accomplished through an ensouled body.[69] Because elevation of soul and denigration of body undermines the gospel's transforming effects on the whole person, Christians must think better of the body.

Explicitly, a lifestyle of embodied holiness can never coexist with ascetic aspirations where the body is poorly thought of and treated with contempt. This is a man-made legalism, as Paul attested. Today, believers are tasked with the same calling—to live by a more biblical anthropology, to forsake a disparaging view of the body, and to move toward an equal embrace of body and soul. To that end, a biblical articulation of human constitution now follows.[70]

Anthropological Dualism

Where the body is ignored or disdained and human constitution is inaccurately assessed, embodied holiness will likely be unattainable. As evidenced in the previous

---

[69] See Marc Cortez, *Embodied Souls, Ensouled Bodies: An Exercise in Christological Anthropology and Its Significance for the Mind/Body Debate* (T&T Clark, 2008).

[70] Greer, "Utilization of a Theology," 51–66.

anthropologies, monism and axiological dualism reject critical Christian beliefs. Monism forsakes resurrection and reembodiment as assured, eschatological promises. Furthermore, it cannot provide a right view of the body in the present, as it rejects eternal corporeal significance, which, as we will see, is one of Paul's chief arguments for the body's value.

On the other hand, axiological dualism promotes an elevation of immaterial over material. Because it understands the soul as relating to God, it reckons the body as an objectionable hinderance to the soul. Still, there is one final anthropological consideration that can correct the problems of monism and axiological dualism. It is this conception of human existence as a holistic dualism that fosters a biblical understanding of embodied holiness.

Holistic Dualism. Holistic dualism is the most biblically accurate depiction of human constitution and has been previously explained by several thoughtful believers. In his work *Sōma in Biblical Theology*, Robert Gundry suggests humans are an anthropological duality. Understanding the Old Testament portrayal of humans as a unit, he credits Paul with avoiding the Greek influence of his day and touting the human person as a unified whole, like the Hebrew Scriptures. For Anthony

Hoekema, in *Created in God's Image*, *psychosomatic unity* is the preferred descriptor for human nature. Similarly, Stanley Grenz's approach examines a holistic alternative to the dichotomist and trichotomist positions in *Theology for the Community of God*.[71] Each of these renderings reflects what John Cooper seeks to achieve with the term *holistic dualism*. While Cooper is not the first to espouse the concept of holistic dualism, his work remains the most comprehensive on the topic. As his description is essential to an embodied view of holiness and one that rightly conceives the body, we must consider it in some detail.

The term "holistic dualism" allows for the twin human realities of a functional holism and an anthropological dualism. Functional holism describes the union of body and soul within a person, whereas anthropological dualism refers to the soul's capacity for existing without the body in the intermediate state.[72] Scripture affirms both. Our eschatological hope rests on the truth of life after death.

---

[71] Robert H. Gundry, *Sōma in Biblical Theology: With Emphasis on Pauline Anthropology* (Cambridge University Press, 1976), 63; Anthony Hoekema, *Created in God's Image*, 217; Stanley Grenz, *Theology for the Community of God* (Eerdmans, 1994), 202–12.

[72] See Cooper, *Body, Soul, and Life Everlasting*, xxvii.

Therefore, further mention of holistic dualism should be understood in the context of anthropological dualism and the survivability of the person, rather than a valuation of soul over body as in axiological dualism. Hence, both views of holism and dualism are essential for understanding embodiment and maintaining a faithful reading of Scripture.

Old Testament Focus. Writers in the Old Testament emphasized humans as whole beings—a functional holism. This emphasis largely arose from the Israelites' understanding of human activity as holistic, evidenced by hundreds of laws involving the body that were imperative to their faith. While some Jewish philosophers believed that the soul was superior to the body, they still advocated the body's health.[73] After all, they recognized that care for the body is care for the soul, and to neglect the body is to neglect the soul. Even if one were to hate his body, his soul still requires attention to it.[74] While this view is certainly not what Scripture advocates, it does support the reality

---

[73] Bahya, *Duties* 8.3, 380.

[74] Smith claims Judaism is "fundamentally an embodied religion." Justin E. H. Smith, *Embodiment: A History* (Oxford University Press), 110.

that embodied humans are psychosomatic entities whose minds and bodies influence each other.

Additionally, the Old Testament frequently utilizes a literary feature called a *synecdoche* to depict human existence. This rhetorical device highlights one part to refer to a whole. Examples of synecdoche can be seen throughout the Old Testament, especially in Wisdom literature. Take, for example, Ps 42:2, where the psalmist declares that his soul desires God. He does not mean that his soul alone is desperate for God; rather, his whole being desires communion with his Maker.[75] In these ways, the Israelites recognized the embodied state and connection of humanity.

New Testament Focus. As for the New Testament, much of the anthropological discussion revolves around the separability of soul from body after death in the intermediate state and before resurrection. Because of Christ's incarnation, fleshly death, and bodily resurrection, the hope his followers have of glorification after death receives much attention. Promises of an afterlife require dualistic construction, so with the Old Testament background of humans as a holism, the New Testament emphasizes the reality of that whole being having two parts. Paul speaks to this twin reality

---

[75] Cooper, *Body, Soul, and Life Everlasting*, 44.

in Phil 1:20–24. Despite his desire to depart and be with Christ, he recognizes it is better for the Philippian believers that he remain in the flesh. Promising that their bodies will be transformed like Christ's body upon resurrection (3:21), Paul states that there is still an intervening period of soul without body, when believers are with the Lord.

Metaphysically speaking, humans are fitted for life in the present age with promises of renewal and restoration for the age to come. The human being is created as a whole entity whose body temporarily separates from soul at death. Sin causes this separation, as the wages of sin is death (Rom 6:23). Because of sin, something must die; for believers, who are rescued from spiritual death, it cannot be the soul. Logically, it must be that the physical life of the body perishes, while the soul and its spiritual life is with Christ, awaiting bodily resurrection.[76] This capacity for separation indicates an ontological distinction between body and soul but need not entail a hierarchical placement of the immaterial over the material.[77]

---

[76] Unbelievers are also resurrected bodily (Acts 24:15) to be judged by the One who will destroy both body and soul in hell (Matt 10:28).

[77] Greer, "The Utilization of a Theology of Human Embodiment to Address Body Image," 68.

Still, this distinction does not interfere with the experience of human embodiment. Humans are unknowable apart from embodied existence. Frankly, it is inconceivable to think of humans without bodies. On earth, the soul cannot express personal qualities apart from the body. In death, the body naturally returns to dust, while the soul goes to the Lord and awaits the time of resurrection and reembodiment. Upon someone's passing, we speak of human constitution differently. Loved ones might refer to the person's "body," signifying the person's immaterial aspect is no longer present. The soul has gone on, while the body remains awaiting resurrection. Soul apart from body is unnatural; likewise, conceiving of a body without a soul is equally illogical.

The post-fall world renders this soul-body division sensible, even essential. Only holistic dualism addresses this compulsory tension in humankind—the tension of a physical and spiritual unity alongside a necessary temporal division between the two. Holistic dualism alone bestows equal honor on the body and the soul and, in doing so, it becomes the only true representation of embodied existence as God intended in a fallen world. Finally, examining a few terms that originate in the Old Testament and extend into the New Testament will give further clarity on the reality of humans as a holistic dualism.

Biblical Terms. While a full biblical anthropology lies outside the scope of this work, four key terms (soul, spirit, heart, and body) require examination, as their usage in the Old Testament informs their meaning in the New Testament.[78] Therefore, the sense behind these terms is important for determining true human nature, which clarifies our understanding of pursuing an embodied holiness.

In the Old Testament, "soul" (Hebrew: *nepeš*) includes a personal meaning in the Hebrew Scriptures. Often translated as "soul" or "life," *nepeš* is the first important term for understanding human nature, and it possesses three main meanings. Soul indicates a living being (Gen 2:7) and is often employed by use of a synecdoche. Next comes the meaning of soul as the life force within a human (Ps 19:7). Its last usage, which is seen in several ways, describes all sorts of internal, unseen activities (Lam 3:20; Job 7:11). Looking at the New Testament, *psychē*, the Greek term for the soul, is similarly used to denote the whole "person" (Rom 12:1), one's core being (Luke 1:46), or the inner life of an embodied being (Eph 6:6).[79]

---

[78] Cooper, *Body, Soul, and Life Everlasting*, 39–49.

[79] Beck and Demarest, *Human Person in Theology*, 131. The LXX used *psychē* as well (131).

The word "spirit" (Hebrew: *rûah*) implies the complete person (Ps 31:5), the life force that God gives (Judg 15:19), an individual's interior life (Exod 28:3), or a person's openness to God (Ps 51:10).[80] The Greek word for spirit is *pneuma*, which is most frequently used by Paul. Its meaning refers to the person (Gal 6:18), the immaterial life force (Jas 2:26), and describes the aspect of humanity that is oriented to God (1 Cor 14:14).

Next, consider "heart" (Hebrew: *leb*), which also frequently appears in the Old Testament and possesses a variety of meanings. While most often rendered as "heart," it also indicates the mind (Ex 14:5), the entire person (Ps 22:26), or inner being (Jer 17:9), among several other usages. The New Testament authors employ *kardia* to specify the center of a person's spiritual and physical life (Rom 6:17) and indicate the mind or the center of one's intellect (Matt 9:4). In these ways, "heart" refers to the wellspring of life, evident in what someone says and does.[81]

In the Old Testament, "body" is most akin to the Hebrew word for flesh, *basar*. Interestingly, some scholars claim the Israelites did not have a distinct word for the body,

---

[80] Gundry, *Sōma in Biblical Theology*, 119.

[81] Beck and Demarest, *Human Person in Theology*, 133–34.

owing to their holistic conception of humanity.[82] *Basar* means the physical body (Gen 2:23), the entire human person (Eccl 4:5), or the weakness or dependency of someone (2 Chr 32:8). Significantly, there is no reference to *basar* as the place of evil or sin.[83] The New Testament uses *sōma* most frequently when it speaks of the material body (Mark 5:29), whole person (Eph 5:28), or the sinful nature (Phil 3:21).[84] Similarly, *sarx* also denotes the body (2 Cor 12:7), human frailty (1 Pet 1:24), and the sinful nature (Rom 8:3–9).[85]

Scripture's use of overlapping anthropological terms resoundingly upends the Platonic and gnostic claims associated with Christian anthropology. Filtering biblical terminology through any philosophical construction

---

[82] Gundry, *Sōma in Biblical Theology*, 117–18.

[83] Beck and Demarest, *Human Person in Theology*, 135.

[84] In Rudolf Bultmann's estimation, *sōma* was not simply a referent to the body but to the whole person. Paul's writing is central to Bultmann's anthropology, and *sōma* lies at the center of Paul's anthropology. Rudolf Bultmann, *Theology of the New Testament*, 2 vols. (Charles Scribner's Sons, 1951–1955), 1:201. While Bultmann's assertion seems correct at first, I believe Gundry accurately represents Paul's intention behind *sōma* when he explains that Paul means to draw attention to the body, the physical entity itself. Gundry, *Sōma in Biblical Theology*, 80.

[85] Beck and Demarest, *Human Person in Theology*, 135.

of humanity that debases the material in favor of the immaterial finds no basis in God's Word. Previous discussion of anti-body philosophies shows that any presumed disparities between the Old and New Testaments were imported into Scripture. The biblical testimony speaks to an embodied being whose disembodiment results from sin but ends in eternal, reembodied life. Now, for a short discussion on the intermediate state for further clarity on this temporary time of unnatural existence, one that is important to understand as we move toward an embodied holiness.[86]

Intermediate State. Belief in the intermediate state is biblically mandated, as the Bible teaches that believers survive death and await resurrection.[87] It is the period after death and before Christ's return when soul and body are disconnected. The believer's remains decompose in the material world, while the immaterial aspect departs to conscious continuation in the presence of Christ (Ps 86:13; 2 Cor 5:8). In this state, disembodiment is a transitory reality. Since believers are saved from spiritual death, physical death remains the passageway into eternity in the new heavens and earth. In the temporary condition of

---

[86] Greer, "Utilization of a Theology," 70–73.

[87] Cooper, *Body, Soul, and Life Everlasting*, 133.

disembodiment, believers wait on the consummation of our promised resurrection and reembodiment.

In 2 Cor 5:1–9, Paul speaks to the coming resurrection and the body's vulnerability to death and decay. He groans in his present body, longing to be with the Lord in a glorious body that is further clothed for his eternal, embodied state, which has surpassed the earthly tent. The indwelling Holy Spirit serves as a promise and guarantee of this complete transformation that begins upon regeneration and fully manifests when glorified believers are further clothed in their resurrection body (Eph 4:30).[88] Bridging this earthly tent and further clothing is a period of disembodied nakedness. So, being unclothed refers to a bodiless soul, an unnatural conception of human nature that is rectified in bodily resurrection.

Importantly, the intermediate state does not debase the body in relation to the soul. In fact, implications of the intermediate state bolster arguments for the body's equivalent value with the soul. Let that sink in. That the body will be glorified proves that the incorporeal person is incomplete, remaining so until reunited with the

---

[88] David E. Garland, *1 Corinthians*, Baker Exegetical Commentary on the New Testament (Baker Academic, 2003), 263.

corporeality. Only holistic dualism, and the compulsory conclusion of an intermediate state, accurately reflects the value Scripture places on the body and thus God's plan for his embodied image-bearers. An influence of anti-body anthropologies must be firmly rejected.

In sum, holistic dualism should be understood as the biblical, logical constitution of humankind. To account for the value of both body and soul while also recognizing the intermediate state, humanity as a holistic dualism stands alone as the singular explanation. This reality should lead Christians to hold soul and body as of equal worth, a critical acknowledgement toward the goal of embodied holiness. After recognizing a description of embodiment in this chapter, we now look to Paul for a Christian conception of the body that will be bolstered by foundational, doctrinal truths.[89]

---

[89] See Greer, "Utilization of a Theology," 74–77.

3

A Theological Argument for the Body

"We are afflicted in every way, but not crushed; perplexed, but not driven to despair; persecuted, but not forsaken; struck down, but not destroyed; always carrying in the body the death of Jesus, so that the life of Jesus may also be manifested in our bodies" (2 Cor 4:8–10). If others are to see Christ in us, then our faith is far more than a spiritual endeavor; it is a biblical expectation to embody holiness.

The apostle Paul and his emphasis on trinitarian involvement with the body are the focus of this chapter. But before diving into the main text for that theological argument from 1 Cor 6:12–20, we must consider unique aspects in Paul's writing—namely, his concept of activity and discussion on the body.

Paul and Physical Activity

Interestingly, Paul weaves a concept of physical activity throughout his writing, the perfect accompaniment to his emphasis on the body. To be sure, pointing out this emphasis does not exclude the contemplative aspect of the Christian life. Scripture clearly expresses God's commands that the believer's thought life be pleasing to him (Phil 4:6–8), to exhibit the mind of the Spirit (Rom 8:5), and to have the mind ready for action (1 Pet 1:13). The point is that Paul's concept of activity supports his frequent conversation on the body, which bolsters a biblical understanding of the body.

Throughout the Pauline letters, Paul's word choice describing Christian responsibility is intriguing, as it suggests physical activity. The decision to use action words like "train," "discipline," "fight," "battle," "beat," "present," "run," "offer," "stand," and "practice" indicates qualities of initiative, intentionality, and self-control in obedience to God. Paul also uses the analogies of a runner, athlete, soldier, and farmer—each one a very physically demanding vocation (1 Cor 9:24–27; 2 Timothy 2). In these ways, he promotes the believer's deliberate, dynamic role in sanctification. As God divinely works, so we work toward holiness as a spiritual and physical being (Phil 2:12–13).

If Christians remain passive regarding aspects of faith, we may lose focus on obedient living, walking by the Spirit, and producing fruit to glorify God. Fallen nature and fleshly habits rule when believers do not engage their minds and bodies in the progress of holiness. This reality makes the need for commands throughout Scripture obvious. Obedient Christianity is an active, participatory calling that extends to all areas of life, even ones that include the body.[1]

As the next section will show, the body comes up a lot in Paul's writing, which renders it an important topic for believers. After a brief description of the historical setting for Paul's letter to the Corinthians, an explanation of 1 Cor 6:12–20 will be given before an outline of trinitarian foundations for a theology of the body.

---

[1] Greer, "The Utilization of a Theology of Human Embodiment to Address Body Image," 214.

Paul and the Body

Because the apostle Paul argues for an embodied approach to holiness, he refers to "the body" time and time again. In fact, he uses *sōma*, Greek for "body," ninety-one times in his epistles to discuss the body, its meaning, and its importance in the Christian life.[2]

So, Christians would do well to contemplate how the body is involved with such doctrinal beliefs as creation, providence, resurrection, the ordinances, and more. As the subject of the body shows up throughout Paul's letters, it is evident that aspects of anthropology, hamartiology, Christology, pneumatology, soteriology, ecclesiology, and eschatology intersect with physical existence. And because

[2] Deborah Beth Creamer, *Disability and Christian Theology: Embodied Limits and Constructive Possibilities* (Oxford University Press, 2009), 46. Paul uses *sōma* in the following verses: Rom 1:24; 4:19; 6:6, 12–13; 7:4–5, 23–24; 8:10–11, 13, 23; 12:1, 4–5; 1 Cor 5:3; 6:13, 15–16, 18–20; 7:4, 34; 9:27; 10:16–17; 11:24, 27, 29; 12:12–20, 22–25, 27; 13:3; 15:35, 37–38, 40, 42, 44, 53; 2 Cor 4:10; 5:6, 8, 10; 7:1, 5; 12:2–3; Gal 6:17; Eph 1:23; 2:3, 16; 3:6; 4:4, 12, 16; 5:23, 28, 30; Phil 1:20; 3:21; Col 1:18, 22, 24; 2:5, 11, 19, 23; 3:5, 15; 1 Thess 4:4; 5:23. In some of these, *sōma* is repeated two or three times. Greer, "Utilization of a Theology," 119.

corporeity is such an important concept to Paul, his discourse on the body serves as the basis for an overarching call toward living embodied holiness.

Equally significant is Paul's metaphorical usage of "body" to describe Christ's church. Think about it: If the body holds no value, then why would Paul associate it with the bride of Christ? Why describe the necessity of each believer's spiritual gifts for the church as the equivalent need of specific parts for the whole body (1 Cor 12:12–31)? Still more, why would he assume care for the body and tie it directly to the care a husband should show for his wife (Eph 5:28–29)? Paul's affirmation of the body throughout his letters starkly contradicts any thinking that discredits the body. As we will see, believers can conclude nothing less than that Paul contended for the body.

Furthermore, Paul's frequent use of body terminology fosters a distinctiveness in his writing. Of special importance is that Paul references the body in a multiplicity of ways to solidify his arguments to Corinthian believers inundated with Greek philosophy that denigrated the material body and elevated the immaterial soul.[3] Utilizing

[3] This axiological dualism prizing soul over body is detailed in chapter 2.

this method, he directly opposes the Corinthians' anti-body tendency throughout his letters.

Paul's body talk comes with implications for the bodies of individual believers along with the church body as a whole. Just as parents have talks with their kids to educate and instruct them, Paul instructs the infantile Corinthians to help them understand the body's significance because their thinking and treatment of the body was so flawed. In the text to be examined, Paul instructs on the proper treatment of the body, which he grounds in proper valuation of the body. His instruction is crucial, as the way we view our body impacts what we do with it. In other words, treating the body well begins with thinking well of the body. As learned from Paul's example, the responsibility of upholding the body's value falls on all believers.

As believers are embodied imagers of God called to do everything for his glory, a devoted, surrendered life is worked out through the body. This reality means Christians value the body, properly conceiving of, stewarding, and preserving it. Thus, the Christian faith reframes all areas of life, particularly actions performed in and with the body, as Paul delineates in 1 Cor 6:12–20. This bodily affirmation is his precise exhortation to the Corinthian believers. To set up Paul's argument for the body, examining the context behind his first letter to the Corinthians is important.[4]

Context of 1 Corinthians

Nowhere is Paul's argument for an embodied view of holiness more evident than in his words in 1 Corinthians. There, he strategically invests in a group of believers living in the prosperous city of Corinth, which was rampant with pagan influences.[5] Ideally situated for trade with other localities, this diverse atmosphere created an influx and resulting acceptance of an assortment of cultural and religious practices, making Corinthian believers highly susceptible to the accommodation of the worldly lifestyles around them, particularly sins of liberality and immorality, which do not seem far off from our contemporary culture.[6]

Likely writing in early AD 54 and having previously interacted with them, Paul knew the Corinthians required

---

[4] Greer, "Utilization of a Theology," 119–22.

[5] Anthony C. Thiselton, *The First Epistle to the Corinthians: A Commentary on the Greek Text*, New International Greek Testament Commentary (Eerdmans, 2006), 1.

[6] Thiselton, *First Epistle to the Corinthians*, 17 (original emphasis removed).

much instruction on Christian living, evidenced by the range of topics he covered. He wrote a few lengthy letters to these believers, some of which were excluded from the biblical canon.[7] Given the lengths of 1 and 2 Corinthians and the existence of other letters, these folks needed both Paul's tutelage and his long-suffering. Paul's writings often include harsh reprimands and detailed explanations, exemplifying the daily concern Paul felt for his churches.[8] Focused on the cross of Christ, his concern was that these Christians know more of the power and wisdom of God, an understanding that was to be applied in all areas of life (1 Cor 1:23–25).

Paul was well educated and familiar with rhetorical techniques to bolster his persuasive argumentation, which his Corinthian audience would recognize from public speeches. Some scholars suggest that Paul worked to refine these strategies, aware that his letters would be read to local congregations.[9] So, his Corinthian arguments often utilize

---

[7] This is the first letter to the Corinthians recorded in the canon of Scripture. As 1 Cor 5:9 attests, Paul had previous dealings with these believers wherein he also confronted their toleration of sexual immorality.

[8] Craig S. Keener, *1–2 Corinthians*, New Cambridge Bible Commentary (Cambridge University Press, 2005), 1.

[9] Keener, *1–2 Corinthians*, 4.

slogans throughout his instruction (6:12–13, 18; 7:1; 8:1, 4–6; 10:23; 11:2).[10] One example is Paul's engagement with an imaginary debater, which he employed by preempting potential Corinthian objections as he built his case for the body.[11]

In chapter 5, after warning against tolerating sexual immorality, Paul exhorts the Corinthians to behave differently from the unbelievers living around them.[12] Like those unbelievers, the Christians apparently felt free to do as they pleased with their bodies, evidenced by the shocking acts of sexual immorality some committed.[13] Contrasting this mindset, Paul declares the body to be the Lord's (6:13)

---

[10] Thiselton, *First Epistle to the Corinthians*, 35.

[11] Keener, *1–2 Corinthians*, 57.

[12] Verlyn D. Verbrugge, *1 Corinthians*, in *1 & 2 Corinthians*, vol 11. of *The Expositor's Bible Commentary*, ed. Tremper Longman III and David E. Garland, rev. ed. (Zondervan, 2017), 246.

[13] Ironically, Martin argues that a faction within the Corinthian church did not consider the body bad but found it inconsequential. Dale B. Martin, *The Corinthian Body* (Yale University Press, 1999), 71. I believe this claim to be similar to the current view of embodied reality within the church. Even if one does not intentionally mistreat the body, apathy and inattention to the body communicate that it does not matter. I harken back to the prevalence of the obesity epidemic in the church.

and, as such, not to be used for sinful pleasures.[14] In a culture that viewed the body as disposable and where all manner of physical vice was justified, Paul's words would have been profound. The worldly-wise philosophers connected the passions of sexual immorality to gluttony, and evidently, the Corinthians did likewise. They justified physical, sexual sins because just as food is made for the body, so also the body is made for sex (6:13).[15] Whereas the believers' conduct in Corinth should have contrasted the depravity on display around them, it unequivocally did not. Things were not as they ought to have been in Corinth. This was the context for Paul's letter.

Another important note of background is the influence of an axiological dualism—a view Paul rejects outright.[16] The Corinthians had split apart the person, conceiving of two disparate aspects: the soul that would last and the body that would perish. Thinking of the body as a mere container for the soul, the Corinthians could live a divided existence where physical matters did not actually matter.

---

[14] Verbrugge, *1 Corinthians*, 310.

[15] Keener, *1–2 Corinthians*, 56.

[16] Robert Scott Nash, *1 Corinthians*, Smyth & Helwys Bible Commentary (Smyth & Helwys, 2009), 175.

Thus, they lived with a false freedom to devote themselves to whatever hedonistic purposes they desired.

With this historical context in place, we now look to the text of 1 Cor 6:12–20, which shows how Paul contrasts the erroneous Corinthian understanding of the body with a proper Christian conception of the body.[17]

Explanation of 1 Corinthians 6:12–20

> *"All things are lawful for me," but not all things are helpful. "All things are lawful for me," but I will not be dominated by anything. "Food is meant for the stomach and the stomach for food"—and God will destroy both one and the other. The body is not meant for sexual immorality, but for the Lord, and the Lord for the body. And God raised the Lord and will also raise us up by his power. Do you not know that your bodies are members of Christ? Shall I then take the members of Christ and make them members of a prostitute? Never! Or do you not know that he who is joined to a prostitute becomes one body with her? For, as it is written, "The two will become one flesh."*

[17] Greer, "Utilization of a Theology," 122–26.

> *But he who is joined to the Lord becomes one spirit with him. Flee from sexual immorality. Every other sin a person commits is outside the body, but the sexually immoral person sins against his own body. Or do you not know that your body is a temple of the Holy Spirit within you, whom you have from God? You are not your own, for you were bought with a price. So, glorify God in your body.*

While this section is in no way meant to be an exhaustive exegesis of 1 Cor 6:12–20, a broad explanation of the text supports my overall claim that a biblical understanding of the body is vital for embodied believers.

Paul's address came amid a dualistic culture that elevated the spiritual over the physical, which led to engagement in sexual immorality. The Corinthian Christians' predominant problem was an errant theology of the body, so they treated the body—and thus their physical actions—as inconsequential. They failed to live as though God rightfully owned the body or as if it possessed any value. So, Paul set out to rectify these pervasive delusions. His pointed statements about trinitarian involvement with the body through the divine works of resurrection, redemption, and indwelling are pivotal to the construction of a theology of the body that leads to an embodied holiness.

Rather than merely chastising the Corinthians for their sins, Paul argues for righteous living on a deeper level. Instead of dishonoring God with the body, he ultimately commands believers to glorify God with their bodies, an overarching call to holy living that he bases on the Trinity. By noting trinitarian involvement with the body, Paul declares the body's value and God's authority over it as the body's rightful owner.

Therefore, this passage is more than a refutation of the sexual sin that ran rampant in Corinth. It is an opposition to an erroneous view of the body. Paul writes to correct the misconceptions that drove the Corinthians' behavior, like the sexual immorality that he flatly condemns. It is true that Paul unequivocally confronts their improper sexual behavior, vehemently denounces their abhorrent acts with prostitutes, and utterly rejects their misunderstanding of freedom in Christ. However, Paul's *core* argument is for the body's value, grounded in the divine works of the Godhead—specifically, the triune acts of resurrection (v. 14), redemption (v. 20), and indwelling (v. 19). Sexual immorality would not have been rampant in Corinth had the Corinthians rightly considered the body. But they failed to, so Paul took aim at the heart of their issues. An explanation of these pivotal verses follows.

Verses 12–14

The licentious Corinthian lifestyle is on full display in 1 Cor 6:12–14, as the hypothetical back-and-forth between Paul and his readers exposes their iniquitous behaviors. In this section, his opening statements are important, as the rhetorical tone of his questioning comes with an obvious answer.[18]

Paul's pointed attack on the Corinthians' mindset and resulting behaviors involves a threefold line of questioning, with the overall goal of reforming how they viewed the body. He counters three presumable Corinthian assertions (vv. 12a, 12c, 13), the first two of which likely misrepresented his prior teaching. The first misunderstanding involved the belief that all things are *permissible* (v. 12a), evoking Paul's counterresponse that *not* all things are *helpful* (v. 12b). In this case, discerning what is permissible requires a determination to avoid sin with a disciplined mindset against sinful behaviors. Paul does not simply

[18] Nash, *1 Corinthians*, 166.

mean freedom from sin but a freedom to live for the Lord, to be intentionally and wholly devoted to him.

The first line of questioning is followed by the second apparent Corinthian misunderstanding that all things are *lawful*. Paul resists this thinking by stating that *nothing* should enslave them (v. 12c).[19] Rather than enslavement, Paul advocates for a moral principle. Anything that could dominate believers, even if not obviously sinful, must be viewed as impermissible and be fought.[20] With a regenerated nature, victory over the former domination of sin is possible. So, believers ward off not only overt sins but also the embedded thinking that leads to enslaving thoughts and behaviors. Paul sought this correction for the Corinthians, one that comes with a variety of applications for embodied believers today.

Discerning the third Corinthian misunderstanding is more challenging. It consists of two parts. The first comment includes an ethical statement (v. 13a), while the following gives evidence of the Corinthians' reasoning

---

[19] Charles H. Talbert, *Reading Corinthians: A Literary and Theological Commentary*, rev. ed., Reading the New Testament (Smyth & Helwys, 2003), 45.

[20] David E. Garland, *1 Corinthians*, Baker Exegetical Commentary on the New Testament (Baker Academic, 2003), 231.

behind it (v. 13b).[21] Essentially, this phrase could promote the thought that all bodily conduct is acceptable because the body will perish anyway. Sexual intercourse and eating were seen as natural aspects of human existence. In both cases, physical satisfaction was sought through seemingly neutral means.[22] Because the Corinthians felt the body was merely temporal and possessed no eternal destiny or purpose, they engaged in sexual immorality.[23] But Paul directly counters this misconception, championing the body's ultimate purpose for the Lord. Thus, believers must not dismiss the body, use it licentiously, abuse it with excess, or disgrace it by a deliberate, immoral lifestyle. Rather, the body is for the Lord and is to be submitted to him in every thought and deed. With this singular truth, Paul calls the

---

[21] Talbert, *Reading Corinthians*, 46.

[22] Talbert, 46.

[23] The Corinthians denial of bodily resurrection "was probably accompanied by an eschatological view that said believers experienced a spiritual resurrection at the moment they believed or were baptized. But in the Corinthians' view, believers were to expect no future bodily resurrection." Andreas J. Köstenberger, L. Scott Kellum, and Charles L. Quarles, *The Lion and the Lamb: New Testament Essentials from "The Cradle, the Cross, and the Crown"* (B&H, 2012), 197.

Corinthians to reevaluate everything they once permitted, in pursuit of an embodied holiness.

Moreover, because the Lord is for the body, Paul declares that it will not be abandoned in death. Just as Christ was resurrected, Paul teaches the promise of future bodily resurrection (v. 14).[24] One way God demonstrated the body's worth is by resurrecting Christ, a miraculous event that ensures the physical resurrection of his followers.

Just as resurrection validates the body, so the Lord is for the body. It is given to him as his right, presently in this world and in the age to come. God creates humans as embodied beings and will resurrect them as embodied beings. And because our present embodied form foreshadows our future reembodied form, what the Corinthians did with their bodies mattered to their faith.[25]

---

[24] I agree with Geisler on numerical identity pertaining to resurrected bodies. As Christ "was raised immortal in the same physical body in which he died," so believers' bodies will be the same, raised in glorious transformation like that of Christ. Norman L. Geisler, *The Battle for the Resurrection* (Thomas Nelson, 1989). Also see, James T. Turner Jr., *On the Resurrection of the Dead: A New Metaphysics of Afterlife for Christian Thought* (Routledge, 2018), 63.

[25] Thiselton, *1 Corinthians*, 94.

Thus, disregard for the body by sexual immorality, sinful indulgence of food, or neglect of body stewardship all demonstrate irreverence for the God of created and resurrected bodies. Each act forsakes the fact that the body belongs to and will be resurrected by him. In these first few verses, Paul clarifies God's authority over the body as established in the promise of future resurrection.

Verses 15–17

Continuing his argument for the proper use of the body, Paul uses the analogy of marital faithfulness to describe the believer's union with Christ. He supplements the analogy with a metaphorical contention that the bodies of Christians are the members, or body parts, of Christ himself. Clearly, a deep union exists between embodied believers and Christ, who remains embodied, an oft-overlooked reality.

Also important, the word "joined" can be interpreted as the act of continually clinging to something (1 Cor 6:16). By using this term, Paul confronts the abhorrent Corinthian choice to leave the Lord and cleave to prostitutes.[26] Believers are united to Christ in such a way that

---

[26] Talbert, *Reading Corinthians*, 49.

to profane the body by engaging in sexual immorality is to reject membership with Christ.[27] Still, there is another significant point to Paul's argument. Based on his rhetorical line of questioning, the implication is clear: Believers' bodies, which are Christ's members, are not available for membership with another.[28] Such intolerable behavior originated from misunderstanding the body's significance.

Furthermore, Paul's mention of Gen 2:24 in v. 16 emphasizes his analogy in a profound way. Wed to Christ, it is impermissible for Christians to withdraw their members from him for union with a prostitute. Believers experience a spiritual, marital union with Christ (v. 17). Thus, to snatch one's members away from Christ and then engage in sexual immorality with another commits a double error: It is an affront against one's own body and an adulterous act directly against the Lord.[29] Thus, in these verses, Paul establishes God's authority over the body and its value in the body's status as united with Christ.

---

[27] Constantine R. Campbell, *Paul and Union with Christ: An Exegetical and Theological Study* (Zondervan Academic, 2015), 302.

[28] Campbell, *Paul and Union with Christ*, 303.

[29] Campbell, 304.

Verse 18

Continuing the renunciation of the Corinthians' unholy behaviors in 1 Cor 6:18, Paul gives a strong command for them to flee immoral behaviors.[30] Some scholars argue that "other" was included to make this verse sensible, whereas without it Paul would contradict himself.[31] If the second part of the verse is seen as another slogan, then it becomes clear that, because they hold the body is unimportant, the Corinthians believe bodily actions are not sinful.[32] Thus, their slogan contends that sin holds no consequence for the

---

[30] Talbert, *Reading Corinthians*, 50. Denny Burk believes 1 Cor 6:18b includes another Corinthian slogan along with the slogans in vv. 12–13. In 1 Cor 6:12–20, Paul utilizes diatribe to form his argument. By doing so, he interacts with an imaginary opponent and includes opposing comments that he expects from the Corinthians. Paul changes the diatribe to engage various slogans by using an oppositional participle along with a counter comment. Denny Burk, "Discerning Corinthian Slogans through Paul's Use of the Diatribe in 1 Corinthians 6:12–20," *Bulletin for Biblical Research* 18, no 1 (2008): 110.

[31] In Burk's understanding, those who insert "other" do so to make sense of the verse and do not render it as another Corinthian slogan. Burk, "Discerning Corinthian Slogans," 111.

[32] Burk, "Discerning Corinthian Slogans," 118.

body. Paul passionately repudiates this ridiculous notion, as sin is an affront to the whole embodied person. Hence, to misuse the body in this way lies outside the bounds of God's created order and intent for embodied holy living.

Verse 19

Previously, Paul referred to the Corinthian believers as a temple (1 Cor 3:16–17), a reference that carries a corporate meaning. As the church, believers are indwelt by the Spirit and thus holy. Now, in 6:19, Paul declares that the individual believer is a temple of the Spirit to highlight God's expectation of bodily purity.[33] As a temple of the Spirit, the believer's body is significant; for where God's Spirit dwells, there his presence resides. Likewise, the body should be regarded as good and holy, as the Father regards his beloved children to whom he gave the Spirit.[34]

Housing and communicating God's presence through embodied existence should motivate believers toward an

---

[33] Campbell, *Paul and Union with Christ*, 290.

[34] John W. Kleinig, *Wonderfully Made: A Protestant Theology of the Body* (Lexham, 2021), 92.

active, continual pursuit to maintain the purity conveyed by identification with the Spirit. Paul's use of rhetoric reminded the Corinthians that they had the Spirit only by God. God had stamped their bodies with his presence. Had the Corinthians really forgotten that fact? Evidenced by Paul's tone, the obvious answer was no.

Paul's confrontation challenges both misuse of and contamination of the body. While united to Christ, to choose to unite oneself to a prostitute is obviously a direct misuse of one's body (v. 15). The issue of contamination is also pertinent. Given that the body is the Spirit's temple, Paul decries the defiling acts of sexual immorality. Such sins that contaminate the body also contaminate the temple and must be resoundingly condemned.[35]

So, in yet another way, God establishes the body's value and his authority over it by blessing it with the presence of the indwelling Holy Spirit (v. 19). With the Spirit's work of indwelling the body, embodied believers have additional motivation to honor God in their actions. Their bodies serve as God's beacon, a light that ought not be darkened by unholy activities.

---

[35] Nash, *1 Corinthians*, 164.

Verse 20

In verse 20, Paul labels embodied believers as Christ's property because God bought them from sin's enslavement. Purchased by Christ's blood and made slaves of God, Christians and their bodies are God's property. Paul places undeniable value on the body with this connection to Christ's act of redemption.[36] Christ charged his people to his care by paying the ultimate price for their embodied lives. Though the cost of redemption was great, it bought a people who are called to glorify God in every area of life, spiritual and physical. Were corporeity not considered an essential element of the Christian faith, the Corinthians would have been justified in giving their bodies to whatever illicit activities they desired. Obviously, this was not the case, and Paul's argument unequivocally condemned it.

Moreover, the command to "glorify God in your body" conveys the message that the body is an instrument, one that can be used to either honor or dishonor God. While holding to holistic dualism, here Scripture presents the

---

[36] Keener, *1–2 Corinthians*, 58.

body as a vessel to steward for the glory of God.[37] As such, Christians ought not to willfully mistreat or neglect their bodies; this calls for physical choices to be scrutinized. Actions done in, by, and with the body require wisdom. The freedom that Paul reframes for the Corinthians is driven by a wise consideration of all things pertaining to bodily life.

Summary of 1 Corinthians 6:12–20

Paul's compendium on the body in 1 Cor 6:12–20 is one of the most important texts, if not the paramount passage,

---

[37] Scripture speaks to the body, at times, with instrumental language, seemingly to specify the principled physical intent that Christian living demands. Believers are to use their bodies to glorify God (1 Cor 6:20) and to present their members not to sin as instruments of unrighteousness but to God as instruments of righteousness (Rom 6:12–13). Other passages emphasize the body as part of a holistic dualism. Believers are commanded to present their bodies to God, which is a spiritual act of worship (Rom 12:1). This verse is a physical command that encompasses the spiritual. In 3 John 2, the apostle indicates that spiritual health is connected to physical health. While care must be taken to avoid non-holistic dualism, it is necessary to reflect biblical language by speaking of the body as an instrument that the Christian is to steward and surrender for the glory of God.

on physical life. Paul champions the body as he highlights three works of trinitarian connection to the body—resurrection, redemption, and indwelling. Additionally, Paul weaves ten explicit truths about corporeal existence throughout these verses:

1. Verse 12: Bodies are not meant to be enslaved to dominating passions.
2. Verse 13: Bodies belong to the Lord.
3. Verse 13: Bodies are meant for the Lord.
4. Verse 14: Bodies will be raised.
5. Verse 15: Bodies are members of Christ.
6. Verse 17: Bodies are joined to the Lord.
7. Verse 19: Bodies are temples of the Spirit.
8. Verse 19: Bodies are owned by God.
9. Verse 20: Bodies are redeemed, along with our souls, by Christ's atonement.
10. Verse 20: Bodies are instruments for glorifying God.[38]

To summarize this section on vv. 12–20, a similar list that compiles Paul's assertions for a theology of the body

---

[38] Lainey Greer, *Struggling with Body Image: Seeing What God Sees* (New Growth, 2024), 39.

is helpful, as it also speaks to embodied reality and body stewardship:

1. He counters gnostic beliefs that dignified the soul and disparaged the body.
2. He contends for God's total authority over the body.
3. He establishes the human body in the external works of the triune God.
4. He calls for bodily purity.
5. He highlights resurrection, redemption, and indwelling to dignify the physical existence.
6. He instructs Christians to live differently from unbelievers, which is typified through bodily conduct.
7. He writes that future resurrection should inform present physical actions.
8. He reminds us that union with Christ includes spiritual benefits.
9. He extends union with Christ to the bodies of believers.
10. He offers foundational instruction on Christian living.

11. He shows that freedom in Christ lies within the bounds of glorifying God with the body.

Additionally, Paul's admonition that the Corinthian believers glorify God in their bodies lays the foundation for the argument that connects holiness with physical well-being. Leading up to that supreme command, his case for physical life can be summarized in two chief declarations: (1) The body has value, and (2) God has authority over it. The body ought not be debased in licentious living, and the Corinthians were not to treat their bodies as if they were their own. So, the command to glorify God in their bodies carries weight for how believers think about and treat their bodies. It is the language of stewardship, of managing the body well in ways that reflect the responsibility given from the Creator God to his embodied beings. In glorifying God with the body, believers assess beliefs, thoughts, and actions that pertain to the body. Living for God's glory through corporeal existence must surely encompass the responsible stewardship of physical health in the pursuit of holiness.[39]

---

[39] Greer, "Utilization of a Theology," 126–36.

Were the body subordinate to the soul or the source of sin, it would not be such a frequent referent for Paul or so intentionally linked by him to analogies in key doctrines. It is this bodily emphasis—seen most notably in his writings to Corinthian believers who lived amid a very gnostic, libertine culture—that renders his focus on trinitarian involvement with the body of particular significance. With this context in place, we now turn to Paul's articulation of a theology of the body in 1 Cor 6:12–20. It is this doctrinal conception of the body that should drive our thinking and push out any remaining anti-body tendencies.

Theology of the Body Foundations

Delineation of a theology of the body from 1 Cor 6:12–20 relies on the fundamental observation that Paul highlights the appropriated works of the Trinity to prove his argument for the body's value. His method is critical, as it bolsters his chief claims. Paul grounds the body's worth in the Godhead by emphasizing the trinitarian works of resurrection, redemption, and indwelling. By this method, he also describes God's authoritative rights over the body and declares its consequent value. In essence, Paul demonstrates various ways that the three persons of the Trinity are involved with the bodily realities of redeemed believers: the promise to embodied believers of a bodily resurrection secured by the Father, the purchase of embodied believers through the redemption achieved in the Son's bodily atonement, and the placement of the indwelling Holy Spirit within embodied believers for holy living. Through these works, the Godhead declares the body's value and God's authority over it, affirming embodied existence with specificity of personhood.[40]

Classical trinitarian doctrine affirms that the three persons possess a singular divine essence while also being differentiated by their eternal relations of paternity, generation, and procession, along with varied roles of creation, redemption, and re-creation.[41] Each person of the Trinity

---

[40] While operating inseparably, each person of the Trinity is specifically involved with the human body. These united but differentiated (or appropriated) works—resurrection, redemption, indwelling—are what I note as specific interactions with physical existence that highlight each divine person's role vis-à-vis the body.

[41] Gregg R. Allison, *The Baker Compact Dictionary of Theological Terms* (Baker, 2016), s.v. "Trinity."

has specific roles and functions, but all work inseparably together toward a divinely established *telos*.[42]

Inseparable operations and specific appropriations are critical aspects of classical trinitarian doctrine and are important to the Pauline text under consideration. The doctrine of inseparable operations states that every divine act is undivided, accomplished in perfect unity from the shared divinity and mutual indwelling of Father, Son, and Spirit.[43] Also essential to trinitarian doctrine—and critical to Paul's theology of the body—is the attendant principle of appropriations, which indicates that each divine work terminates in one of the persons of the Godhead.[44] Certain activities in the world, while involving inseparably the other two persons, can be attributed or specified to one person.[45] Appropriations are in keeping with the eternal relations of the Father, Son, and Holy Spirit and include a specific

---

[42] Michael Horton, *Rediscovering the Holy Spirit: God's Perfecting Presence in Creation, Redemption, and Everyday Life* (Zondervan, 2017), 58.

[43] Gregg R. Allison and Andreas J. Köstenberger, *The Holy Spirit*, Theology for the People of God (B&H Academic, 2020), 281.

[44] Allison and Köstenberger, *Holy Spirit*, 282.

[45] Allison and Köstenberger, 228.

divine work's termination in a particular person. While performed inseparably, the works of resurrection, redemption, and indwelling each terminate in a specific person, validating the argument that Paul grounds the body in the Trinity.

Therefore, this method of explaining a theology of the body is simply borrowed from Paul. He highlights specific divine actions appropriated to specific divine persons for two central purposes—to demonstrate God's authority over the believer's body and to affirm the value of the body. By this method, Paul opposes a culture and its behaviors that were, at best, apathetic and, at worst, antagonistic to the human body. The divine works of resurrection, redemption, and indwelling function as a combined reinforcement to bolster his claims about the body. Paul emphasizes these works before commanding that the Corinthians honor God in their bodies. His clear purpose and progression cannot be overstated for our own setting. Christians today must allow these deep, doctrinal beliefs about our bodies to inform what we do with them. To lay more of that doctrinal groundwork, we will investigate the appropriated works that Paul stressed.

The next sections offer a deeper explanation of the specific ways the Godhead affirms the body: the Father's work in resurrection and creation, the Son's work of redemption and his embodied example, and the Spirit's work of indwelling and the fruit of self-control. These trinitarian connections to the body signify its value and God's authority over it.[46]

Resurrection

The first trinitarian work in Paul's treatise that confirms the body's significance is resurrection, a divine act that defines the body's worth while also asserting God as its rightful owner. The body itself is esteemed in the promise of future resurrection.[47] If Christians were better off bodi-

---

[46] Greer, "Utilization of a Theology," 136–40.

[47] Richard Hays explains:

> No one who understands the fundamental content of the kerygma can suppose that our bodies are irrelevant. The body is not simply a husk to be cast off in the next life; the gospel of Jesus Christ proclaims that we are to be redeemed body, soul, and spirit. Salvation can never be understood as escape from the physical world or as the flight of the soul to heaven. Rather, the resurrection of the body is an integral element of the Christian story. Those who live within that story, then, should understand that what they do with their bodies in the present time is a matter of urgent concern.

less or the body were a useless container for the soul, then why gloriously resurrect it? But with the same power that raised Christ, believers are promised a glorified body and perfected embodiment.

Furthermore, eternal embodied existence should guide temporal embodied conduct. Paul emphasizes this point to the Corinthians, who misunderstood the body and its future—a delusion that spawned licentious living, abuse of the body, and dishonor toward its divine owner in their present. While the Father, Son, and Spirit inseparably operate in all external works, resurrection terminates in the Father and is one of Paul's main statements of trinitarian involvement with the body.[48]

Richard B. Hays, *First Corinthians*, Interpretation: A Bible Commentary for Teaching and Preaching (Westminster John Knox, 2011), 104.

[48] Scripture speaks of each person of the Trinity as involved in resurrection (John 10:18; Rom 8:11; Gal 1:1), but Paul specifies it to the person of the Father most frequently and explicitly in Acts 2:32; Rom 6:4; and Gal 1:1. I believe it is fitting to engage in the detailed investigation of resurrection and attribute it to the Father, like Kyle Claunch, who advocates a broad and detailed investigation of divine actions per the inseparability principle alongside appropriations. Kyle Claunch, "What God Hath Done Together: Defending the Historic Doctrine of the

Resurrection is a pivotal Christian belief, for if Christ has not been raised, then believers are still in their sin (1 Cor 15:17). Without it, Christianity would be a sham, because apart from Christ's resurrection, believers are left hopeless (1 Cor 15:19). But as the Father raised the Son from the dead, so also will the Father raise Christ's followers from the dead (Rom 8:11; 1 Cor 6:14; Gal 1:1). Rising from the dead as the firstfruits, Christ secured redemption for those who believe in him (1 Cor 15:20). Though believers who physically die are disembodied for a time, this redemption guarantees bodily resurrection and glorification (15:23, 42–44).[49] It was of extreme importance to Paul that the Corinthians believed that resurrection was not simply a spiritual occurrence (15:12, 35). From the influence of Gnosticism, the Corinthians surmised that

---

Inseparable Operations of the Trinity," *Journal of Evangelical Theological Society* 56, no. 4 (December 2013): 795. Therefore, the underlying endeavor in my theology of the body simply engages in this detailed investigation of the divine actions of resurrection, redemption, and indwelling, which undergirds Paul's articulation of trinitarian involvement with the body.

[49] As discussed in chapter 2, the state of disembodiment will not last. In the intermediate state, the perishable body awaits its resurrection to imperishability, a reuniting of body and soul where this glorified embodiment eternally endures.

physicality was objectionable, which impacted their belief in a physical resurrection.[50] So, they lacked motivation for moral living because they errantly thought that only spiritual things mattered. They mistreated the body because they hated it, believing there was no use for it. In doing so, they pursued a disembodied holiness, completely neglecting a fundamental piece of the Christian faith.

To remedy the Corinthians' problematic portrayal of their current bodies, Paul discusses its connection to the future body. While the heavenly body possesses a specific glory of its own, the earthly body also has a certain kind of glory and, therefore, is not disposable. Paul gives three analogies to distinguish the two bodies: a seed and plant; animal flesh and human flesh; and the sun, moon, and stars (1 Cor 15:37–41).

With these three comparisons, Paul differentiates the heavenly body from the earthly body without diminishing present corporeality. He maintains the earthly body's value with the proclamation of an eternal embodiment. This truth means that the Corinthians' present actions were important. Because the body will be transformed to

---

[50] Thomas R. Schreiner, *New Testament Theology: Magnifying God in Christ* (Baker Academic, 2008), 854.

"bear the image of the man of heaven" (1 Cor 15:49), believers should be motivated to honor Christ in their bodies now.[51]

Once resurrected, Christians will experience embodiment in a new way.[52] Yes, we await a spiritual inheritance of all blessings in Christ in the heavenly realms (Eph 1:3). But there are additional untold blessings ahead in the new heavens and new earth, ones that require a physical existence to experience the material wonders in God's re-created, sinless physical world.

In our future embodied existence, we will enjoy a freedom from sin's multifaceted manifestations, like physical deformity, blindness and deafness, cognitive impairment,

---

[51] Stephen J. Wellum, *God the Son Incarnate: The Doctrine of Christ*, Foundations of Evangelical Theology (Crossway, 2016), 229.

[52] Eric L. Johnson, *God and Soul Care: The Therapeutic Resources of the Christian Faith* (IVP Academic, 2017), 551. Interestingly, Wayne Grudem connects the pursuit of physical health in this age with the lasting state of physical health in the age to come. Concluding that future resurrection proves that God is concerned with the present condition of the body, he comments that Christians should seek to be in good health now. Wayne Grudem, *Christian Ethics: An Introduction to Biblical Moral Reasoning* (Crossway, 2018), 659.

and other physical abnormalities that disrupt daily functioning. While lacking details on the resurrected body's appearance, Paul foreshadows key differences between the future and present body (1 Cor 15:42–44). We learn the believer's risen form will be imperishable, glorious, powerful, and spiritual. The body will be eternal, never again threatened by death and decay. It will be glorious, no longer marked by the shame and stain of sin. It will be powerful, being fully restored to God's image. Finally, the future body will experience complete surrender to the Holy Spirit.[53]

Outside of 1 Corinthians 15, Romans 8 is another key passage on resurrection. Having promised that believers will be raised with their mortal bodies, receiving new life (Rom 8:11), Paul links the restoration of all created, physical things to the redemption of the physical body (vv. 19–23). Here, Paul reassures believers that creation will not be left as it is but will be remade. This teleological promise unites Christ, his followers, and all of creation, over which he is supreme. Paul mentions bodily renewal to help believers recognize that this restoration will involve the body. A re-created, physical creation will be inhabited by

---

[53] Gregg R. Allison, *Embodied: Living as Whole People in a Fractured World* (Baker, 2021), 256.

reembodied, physical believers. Even more, "the redemption of our bodies" seems to explain what "our adoption as sons" will entail (v. 15). What Paul clarifies here is that the believer's adoption is not complete until the resurrected body is attained.[54]

As the resurrection clearly confirms the body's value and assures believers of future embodiment, its implications for our present life and embodied living are vast. But just as resurrection entails restoring life, it also harkens back to our Creator God, the One who gives life. Creation is a work that explicitly expresses God's authority. The Creator has supreme authority over his creation, and in this Creator-creature distinction, God's unlimited power and transcendent qualities are evident. His control and authority over all things reveals that his power is manifested throughout time and space, ordering all things by his command.[55] And while creation is appropriated to the Father, it is important to note that the Son and Spirit are also active, working inseparably in this divine work (Gen 1:1–2; Col 1:15–16).

---

[54] Johnson, *God and Soul Care*, 551.

[55] John M. Frame, *The Doctrine of God*, A Theology of Lordship (P&R, 2002), 293.

Taken one step further, as Paul does in 1 Cor 6:12–20, creation—along with redemption and indwelling—establishes God's ownership of the body. The creation of God's embodied image-bearers must be examined, as it is critical to a theology of the body. With Paul's reference to Genesis 2 in 1 Cor 6:16, it may be that he had the created body in mind while he wrote of the resurrected body. Connecting the creation of embodied imagers to the resurrection of those same embodied imagers proves God's authority over the body while also verifying its value.

Created in the Imago Dei

Resurrection clearly links to creation, as he who resurrects life must be the One who establishes it. Toward the goal of embodied holiness, Christians understand that humans are distinctly created to reflect God. He designed living creatures according to their kinds, like birds, fish, and livestock (Gen 1:21–25). However, when God created the first humans, he fashioned them after his likeness for the purpose of bearing his image and fulfilling his commands.[56]

---

[56] Irenaeus referred to humanity as a "mixed organization of soul and flesh (body), who was formed after the likeness of God

Without bodies, God's creation commands of procreation and vocation are impossible. In the first responsibility of procreation, Adam and Eve were to be fruitful and multiply, to fill the world with God's image-bearers (4:1–2, 25). Their descendants continue to fulfill this responsibility (5:1–32), but God's plan did not stop with procreation. God's embodied image-bearers are also designed to fulfill his second creation command of vocation. This responsibility means that men and women express dominion over creation as they lovingly subdue and steward all that God created. The care that God's imagers show for creation involves tending to his physical works, like animals, plants, and even the body. The body is part of God's creative activity and comes with the expectation of reverent stewardship, a management that attends to health and well-being.

Thus, the corporeal form is integral to the way humans are created to function.[57] Being embodied, we carry out God's creation commands in our requisite image-bearing

and molded by His hands—that is by the Son and Holy Spirit, to whom also He said, 'Let Us make man' (Gen 1:26)." Irenaeus of Lyon, *Against Heresies* 4, preface, para. 4 (*ANF* 1:463).

[57] For more on the fundamentals of humans as created in the image of God, see Bruce K. Waltke, *Genesis: A Commentary* (Zondervan Academic, 2001), 65–66.

form. So, body and soul constitute the image of God and are equally valued. Even more, if one's corporeal frame was insignificant or wicked, then surely physical matter would not be a fundamental aspect of humanity. Were the body an incidental vessel for the soul, why esteem it with the *imago Dei*? But as we have seen, Scripture testifies otherwise. Creation then, traditionally appropriated to the Father and naturally tied to resurrection, is essential to a properly conceived theology of the body.

Though every part of God's creation is deemed good, only humankind is bestowed with the title of imager. This is a position of honor, a momentous designation for humanity not to be overlooked or ill-conceived. Otherwise, the value of the human being is up for debate, the body in particular.[58] Disregard for the *imago Dei* nullifies human dignity, responsibility, personhood, and ethics. Without this vital connection between the person and the body, God's Word is rejected, and all manner of ill treatment becomes permissible. Any perverse, God-denying act against the body can be justified: abortion, sexual immorality, homosexuality, gender-affirming surgeries, euthanasia, bestiality,

---

[58] Nancy R. Pearcey, *Love Thy Body: Answering Hard Questions About Life and Sexuality* (Baker Books, 2018), 26.

pedophilia, acts of self-harm, and other worldly methods of destruction. Christians, then, must recognize the significance of bearing the *imago Dei*, its extension into daily life, and its meaning for rightly viewing the body.[59]

As the Father's affirmation of the body is foundational to embodied holiness, the Son's involvement with the body provides additional clarity on its worth and purpose.[60]

---

[59] Salvation partially restores God's image in this life but fully in the life to come. Though it was marred in the fall (Gen 3), the image was not destroyed in sinful humanity (Gen 9:6). It can be renewed in Christ, who is the image of the invisible God (Col 1:15). Christ, the perfect image, restores the image of God in redeemed men and women—a reality that bears fundamental importance for the overall meaning of the image. Christ secures future restoration of the *imago Dei* in his followers (Rom 8:29; 2 Cor 3:18). He came to the earth to live, die, and live again to secure this teleological promise through salvation. Believers, then, live by the Spirit to progress in holiness, putting on the new self, and experiencing progressive conformity to the image of our Creator (Col 3:9–10). For discussion on the image of God and Christ, who is the perfect image of God, see Allison, *Embodied*, 124. See also Marc Cortez, *ReSourcing Theological Anthropology: A Constructive Account of Humanity in the Light of Christ* (Zondervan Academic, 2018), 99–130.

[60] Greer, "Utilization of a Theology," 140–49.

Redemption

Continuing with his trinitarian proofs in 1 Cor 6:12–20, Paul cites the Son's act of redemption as further evidence of God's authority over the body and the validity of its worth. Mentioning specific bodily implications of the believer's union with Christ, he reminds the Corinthians that they were bought at the high price of Christ's bloody, bodily work of atonement. His sacrificial payment secured the purchase of embodied believers, who are united in an embodied membership with him (1 Cor 6:13, 15–17, 19). Paul pointedly declares to the anti-body Corinthians that their very bodies are included in redemption. To be sure, the Son's willing condescension and torturous death on behalf of his embodied followers undoubtedly indicates the body's value. And because the body cannot be excluded from what Christ redeemed, it must also not be excluded from endeavors to grow in Christlikeness.

As sinners, we require redemption from sin in soul and body. Every part of our humanity experiences corruption and depravity, so the scope of redemption cannot be limited to spiritual matters alone. But this was the Corinthians' problem. Denying the body as part of what will be fully redeemed was a grave error and one that excused hedonistic conduct. Because Paul condemned the thinking that allowed them to do as they pleased physically, redemption is another proof of God's authority over the body. He paid for it with his blood; thus, the Corinthians' only response should have been to glorify him in those bodies (v. 20).

In 1 Cor 6:12–20, Paul's repeated and simultaneously nuanced emphases on material nature, its value, and God's power over it should not be surprising, particularly when it is the same nature that Christ assumed. Being obedient to the Father and sustained by the Spirit, the Son humanly suffered and humanly died. Per Athanasius, he took on a body that is able to die.[61] So, Christ's embodied form functioned as the means of redeeming sinful, embodied humans. Therefore, the incarnate Son's physicality is essential to Christology.

Because embodiment is the natural state of human experience, heresy is born from a denial of Christ's embodiment (see 1 John 1:1; 4:3). As previously discussed, it is imperative to realize that an inaccurate appraisal of Christ's physical existence jeopardizes his atoning work and, thus, the gospel. Christ's role as an embodied human is necessary for each aspect of his work—incarnation, life, death,

---

[61] Athanasius of Alexandria, *On the Incarnation*, trans. John Behr, Greek-English ed. (St. Vladimir's Seminary Press, 2011), 9.

resurrection, and ascension. Recognizing that the Son's physicality is essential to redemption, believers should deem Christ's embodiment significant for their own. We value our own bodies as a critical part of present Christian life while holding to the certainty of bodily renewal in eternity.

Christ was also an embodied sacrifice.[62] Physically, he was beaten and pierced, and he thirsted, sweat, and bled. He died because his body could not withstand the cruel, torturous abuse, and it is through his broken body that sinners gain atonement. Without the physical presence of Christ to bodily take humanity's place, satisfy divine wrath against sin, and bear our sin in his body on the tree, redemption is incomplete (1 Pet 2:24). If by his wounds we are healed (Isa 53:6), then the incarnation is mandated for our salvation. His body is a requisite part of the atonement (Gal 4:4–5), rendering Christ's embodied life an example for his followers and informing our pursuit of holiness.[63]

---

[62] This statement is from Gregg R. Allison (personal correspondence to the author, n.d.).

[63] Ivor J. Davidson speaks of the physicality of Christ's fleshy salvation as a fact of history, which sanctifies the human experience of embodiment. He notes that Christ, as the mediator of the redeemed, bears their sins in his body (1 Pet 2:24), sanctifies them by offering his body (Heb 10:10), and cleanses

The necessity of Christ's body is also connected to the reality of physical suffering. As the propagation of the gospel often leads to persecution, the body becomes the canvas for bearing the reproach of Christ. Because the cruciform kingdom is typified in Christ's physical suffering on the cross, believers' bodily suffering for the kingdom is expected.[64] So, the body matters because by it believers follow Christ's example of endurance, understanding the reality that they may be persecuted just as he was (John 15:20). Paul, who through his body shared in Christ's sufferings, aimed to become like him in his death while awaiting glorious, bodily transformation (Phil 3:10, 21). Believers, then, recognize and respect the body as the means of following in Christ's stead. While the avoidance of suffering is attractive, as many false gospels proclaim, looking to Christ's embodied sacrifice secures the believer's

---

them, making peace as his body bleeds on the cross (Col 1:20; 1 John 1:7). Ivor J. Davidson, "Atonement and Incarnation," in *T&T Clark Companion to Atonement*, ed. Adam J. Johnson (T&T Clark, 2017), 45.

[64] Treat explains the cruciform kingdom as dependent upon the centrality of the cross of Christ. Jeremy R. Treat, *The Crucified King: Atonement and Kingdom in Biblical and Systematic Theology* (Zondervan, 2014), 227.

role in the cruciform kingdom. If the importance of the body is lost, so is the meaning of the cross.

Embodied Example

The Son of God became incarnate when he took on human nature to secure the redemption of those God had chosen for salvation before the world began. We know that his body was like all other physical, human bodies. Though mysterious, this truth does not threaten his divinity, which the hypostatic union affirms (John 1:14; Phil 2:6–7; Col 2:9).[65] Jesus experienced a human birth, grew in stature, ate and drank, worked with his hands, got his feet dirty, and physically expired on the cross. He paid the ultimate price, bodily securing redemption for believers by his death and resurrection (see Heb 9:11–12; 10:5). Still, he also ascended to heaven in that same body, now gloriously perfected, where he remains embodied.[66] The body's value is affirmed in the

---

[65] The hypostatic union refers to the joining of two natures, divine and human, in the one man, Jesus Christ. Allison, *Baker Compact Dictionary*, s.v. "hypostatic union."

[66] While his ascension is often overlooked, Christ's resurrection and ascension are equally necessary to his atoning work. Robert Letham poignantly states the reality of Christ's continued

Son's willingness to take on a body, becoming embodied in order to sympathize with our weaknesses (Heb 4:15). Christ's physical body is an essential prerequisite to accomplishing the whole of his redemptive work—incarnation, atonement, resurrection, and ascension. Still, the necessity of his bodily existence between his incarnation and ascension needs further examination for determining how his embodied example should spur us on toward embodied holiness.

Christ's embodied obedience to the Father, carried out after his incarnation and up to his ascension, highlights the same expectation for his followers. Living as an embodied exemplar for his embodied disciples, Christ perfectly fulfills God's command to glorify him in the body. In his atoning work, Christ obediently offers himself, suffering unto death as sinful humanity's sinless substitute. The very ground of his substitution lies in his righteous life as the faithful Son who faultlessly fulfilled his Father's commands. It is only by this righteous life that righteousness can be imputed to sinners who believe in him.

---

embodiment, affirming, "Our human flesh is taken to the right hand of God, invested with the glory of God, and received by the Father." Robert Letham, *Systematic Theology* (Crossway, 2019), 577.

Consequently, with his body as the conduit, Christ expresses a sinless existence, which is necessary for his work of recapitulation.[67] The divine Son had to become a living, breathing man to recapitulate the obedient life that Adam had failed to carry out (Rom 5:12–21). Through his body, he actively keeps the law and passively becomes a curse for those who broke the law. Humbling himself, the divine Son was born in the likeness of man (Phil 2:7) to obey his Father as the last Adam and the only human who could restore what was lost by the first.[68]

Additionally, while on earth, Christ's material tangibility was an essential element to his ministry. Many of Jesus's miracles occurred simply by his speaking, and others were performed through his physical touch. On such occasions, the embodied Christ imparted healing to those suffering as embodied beings. Though he did not need to involve his body to heal their suffering, in doing so, he honors their physicality in the usage of his own.

Consider the following examples. When Peter's mother-in-law is ill, Jesus takes her hand, helps her

---

[67] Treat, *The Crucified King*, 210.

[68] Stephen J. Wellum, *Christ Alone: The Uniqueness of Jesus as Savior*, Five Sola Series (Zondervan, 2017), 163.

up out of bed, and heals her without speaking a word (Mark 1:30–31). He touches a leper, commanding him to be clean (Mark 1:40–42). Matthew tells of a grieving centurion who pleads for Christ to touch his daughter and raise her back to life. Jesus grabs her hand, and she is restored to life (Matt 9:24–26). Just after that, Jesus touches a blind man, healing him through his physicality (Matt 9:28–30). Mark records a miraculous account of when Jesus placed his fingers into a deaf man's ears. After spitting and touching his tongue, Christ remedied the man's speech impediment (Mark 7:32–35). Mark reports that Jesus restores a blind man's sight by spitting on the man's eyes and touching him with his hands (Mark 8:23–25). John describes a similar instance when Jesus heals blindness by applying saliva to a man's eyes (John 9:6–7). Luke reveals a healing of a crippled woman where Jesus declares her free from infirmity and then proceeds to touch her (Luke 13:11–13). Matthew demonstrates Jesus using his body to heal two blind men by touching their eyes (Matt 20:30–34). Luke records when Christ touched the soldier's ear to heal it after a sword-wielding Peter cut it off (Luke 22:50–51). Repeatedly in the Gospels, hurting people plead for Christ's touch to impart the healing they so desperately sought.[69] Physical touch was so significant that it gave the disciples undeniable assurance that Jesus had truly risen from the dead (Luke 24:39).

Moreover, there would be no wilderness temptation without Christ's physical body. If Christ were not flesh and blood, how would Satan have provoked him to alleviate his physical needs (Matthew 4)? To fully sympathize with humanity, it was necessary that he endure physical temptations and yet remain impeccable (Heb 4:15; 5:8). Christ felt hunger and thirst (Mark 11:12; John 19:28). He wept in anguish (John 11:35). He was surely tempted to engage his members as instruments of wickedness instead of righteousness. But he remained sinless in body and mind. In the end, his obedience led to the experience of bodily pain—so torturous that he sweat blood, anticipating the spiritual and physical turmoil ahead.

Christ fulfilled the faithful obedience God requires in his bodily life as a sinless substitute for humans. Thus, it follows that Jesus sets the example of a life wholly devoted to God. Believers look to his embodied existence as the consummate example of complete surrender and strive to follow his embodiment of holiness.

---

[69] A few examples are Matt 9:21; 14:36; Mark 3:10; 8:22; 10:13; and Luke 6:19.

In the end, to neglect the physical nature of Christ's earthly ministry inevitably disregards the material significance of the Christian's earthly life. Because his incarnation through his ascension are historical events that entail a body, they necessitate respect for the body.[70] The Son's assumption of a human nature amplifies the Christian conception of the body and requires us to hold a sound theology of the body. To that end, given the Father and Son's participation with the body, explaining the Holy Spirit's association with it is the next Pauline priority and an important understanding for embodied holiness.[71]

Indwelling

The Holy Spirit and his indwelling presence in believers is Paul's third and final mention of trinitarian involvement

[70] To speak of Christ's human nature and highlight his bodily existence in such ways is to echo Gregory of Nazianzus' rule of partitive exegesis. The point is not to press division between the divine and human natures but to maintain their unity in the God-man, while appreciating how his incarnation informs our view of the body. Gregory of Nazianzus, *The Third Theological Oration* 29.18, https://www.newadvent.org/fathers/310229.htm.

[71] Greer, "Utilization of a Theology," 149–56.

with the body in 1 Cor 6:12–20. Before considering this work, a brief explanation of the Spirit's overall activity is fundamental for grasping the purpose of his presence within believers.

Starting with the creation event, the Spirit's presence is important, as he works inseparably with the Father and Son. In Gen 1:2, he hovers over the waters as the Father speaks created matter into being by the Word (John 1:1–4). The Spirit is sent with the purpose of producing fruit from the newly created materials in accordance with the Father's command (Gen 1:11–12; Ps 104:30).[72] Where all was once formless, void, and dark, life now exists. Vitality and fruit abound because the Third Person of the Trinity perfects what the First and Second Persons of the Trinity create, ever working to compel creation to its divinely designed purpose.[73] In keeping with his agency in creation, the Spirit's work points to his activity in believers and in the new heavens and new earth.

As creation did not spring to life on its own or produce fruit without God, neither do humans. Thus, the Spirit's

---

[72] Abraham Kuyper and Benjamin B. Warfield, *The Work of the Holy Spirit*, trans. Henri de Vries (Cosimo Classics, 2007), 48.

[73] Allison and Köstenberger, *Holy Spirit*, 78, 84.

work in creation reflects his activity in believers, our regeneration and new birth. He regenerates hearts of stone and brings this new birth about in those formerly dead in sin and only able to produce fruits of the flesh (Gal 5:19–21). Life and vitality come about where there was once death and darkness. Through his indwelling presence, the Spirit enables believers to comprehend Scripture and transforms us as we apply it. In this way, he advances us in holiness, purifying and sustaining us until glorification, when he will re-create and perfect all things. As in creation and re-creation, the Spirit will not fail to complete the work initiated by Father and Son.[74] Through his presence, the Spirit securely unites believers in Christ, granting them all the blessings of salvation.[75] Having received the Spirit from God (1 Cor 6:19), believers are empowered for fruit-bearing and advancing in godliness, a divine transformation that involves the body and that will be brought to completion in resurrection.

By his indwelling presence, the body is specifically labeled as the Spirit's temple (1 Cor 6:19). With this

---

[74] Graham A. Cole, *He Who Gives Life: The Doctrine of the Holy Spirit*, Foundations of Evangelical Theology (Crossway, 2007), 74.

[75] Allison and Köstenberger, *Holy Spirit*, 375.

pronouncement, Paul unequivocally confirms the body's value and God's authority over it. This final mention of trinitarian involvement with the body leaves no doubt that God sanctions the body's worth, affirming it with the Spirit's placement. Even more, the Spirit's specific location denotes authoritative ownership of the body. Far more than a shell for the soul, the body is a house for the Spirit.

In specifying the Spirit's placement, Paul clearly calls the Corinthians to pursue holy living and forsake illicit, physical pleasures. The Spirit's very presence condemns immorality and bestows an honor on the body that was foreign to Gnosticism. The Corinthians' bodies are claimed for a higher, eternal purpose, one that the Spirit's dwelling guarantees. So, embodied believers are called to be set apart because we are regenerated by the Spirit, sealed with his presence, and made his temple (1 Cor 6:19; see also Eph 1:13–14). Owned by God in body and soul, we live devoted to him in every way—as his embodied holy image-bearers and vessels of his holy presence within.

It is also worth pointing out that Paul did not need to specify the Corinthians' bodies as the place where the Spirit dwelt. His point would have been well taken had he merely said, you are a temple of the Holy Spirit. But once again, Paul goes out of his way to include the body in the Christian faith, clearly showing its importance to a group of believers who deemed it unimportant. Likewise, equating the believer's body to God's temple denotes the Spirit's continual ability to implant and grow spiritual vitality in his children now.[76] As the temple was God's building, so believers are his possession. For Paul to pronounce *the body*—the very object of Corinthian abuse—as the Spirit's temple should have brought a confidence that, with the Spirit's help, they would be able to glorify God in their bodies.

Linking the Spirit's bodily presence with the temple affords the body an undeniable significance that carries through eternity. Formerly, God dwelt in the temple under the old covenant (Exod 25:8; 40:34), a reality that required laws to ensure purity and holiness. But under the new covenant, the Spirit dwells within believers, who receive his help to live holy lives (Ezek 37:26–28; Rom 8:11; 2 Tim 1:14). Also of significance in the Old Testament is the Holy Spirit's work in the tabernacle and temple building process. The Israelites could not have completed God's aesthetic expectations apart from the divine help that the

[76] Frame, *Doctrine of God*, 598.

Spirit supplied, which produced beautiful, skillful, and fruitful work (Exod 31:1–5). The construction of God's dwelling place in the old covenant highlights that, in the new covenant, his people will one day be made perfect in every way, even their bodies.

As we cannot attain our own righteousness, the Spirit works within us to govern our embodied lives, producing what we lack in body and soul. Thus, the final work concerning the Spirit and the body is sanctification, which plays out as Christians progressively pursue an embodied holiness through the fruit of self-control.

Sanctification and Self-Control

The Holy Spirit sanctifies embodied believers as he dwells in them and supplies his fruit for holy living. Simply put, sanctification is the process of becoming more holy, living more like Christ, and increasing in devotion to God in all areas of life. Traditionally, there are different aspects of sanctification, described as positional, progressive, and perfected. Positionally, believers are declared righteous, being justified by faith. Our position before God is secure in Christ. Progressive sanctification involves our responsibility to grow in holiness. While declared holy, we are still called to be holy as God is holy, which is a continuous process until we are glorified (1 Pet 1:15). Perfected sanctification will be achieved in the eschaton, after resurrection, when the corruption of sin is no more.[77] Knowing these realities, believers should be confident. The Spirit will not fail to accomplish the ends for which he was sent by the Father and Son: the work of conforming believers to Christ (2 Thess 2:13). The Spirit will bring his work to completion.

Comprehending the Spirit's activity is critical to the goal of this book. Embodied reality is evident in the Spirit's role as sanctifier because his work takes place spiritually and physically (see Col 3:2; 1 Thess 4:3–4). His empowering presence supplies Christians with the ability to honor God in every area of life. Because we require transformation in soul and body, the Holy Spirit can change our desires, beliefs, feelings, and action. Humbled by his provision for godly living (2 Pet 1:3), we obey God as he transforms us in soul and body. As we obey, we work out our salvation with humble gratitude, knowing that the ability and desire for godliness is divinely implanted (Phil 2:12–13). In the

[77] Allison and Köstenberger, *Holy Spirit*, 411.

working out of our salvation, we assess what it means to glorify God in all areas of life.[78]

Self-Control

In Galatians 5, Paul explains more about the Spirit's role in the believer's daily life. He presents two distinct ways of

---

[78] Greer, "Utilization of a Theology," 35–36. Moreover, the twin reality of the believer's maturation relies on effort—of the Spirit and of oneself (Phil 1:6; 2:12–13). The twofold effort grounds progressive sanctification: It is God working in us so that we live as he originally intended. Through mortification and vivification, the Spirit helps us put off our old self, renew our minds, and put on the new self (Eph 4:22–24). Mortification is the negative aspect of sanctification, whereby the Spirit slays the old self and its power while the believer battles sin wherever it arises. The positive aspect of sanctification is vivification, whereby the Spirit fortifies the new self while the believer pursues righteousness. Bruce Demarest, *The Cross and Salvation: The Doctrine of Salvation*, Foundations of Evangelical Theology (Crossway, 2007), 403. See also Cole, *He Who Gives Life*, 229. Both movements are enabled by the Spirit and dependent upon the believer's intake of God's Word. Progressing in holiness, Christians surrender to and obey God's commands. In mortification and vivification, the embodied believer can now live a life that is visibly distinct from the world.

living, with no ambiguities. One is by the flesh, exhibiting deeds of the sinful nature. The other comes by the Spirit, exemplifying his fruit. Christians are commanded to walk, be led, and live by the Spirit (Gal 5:16–26). Keeping these commands involves a conscious choice, an intentionality only possible with a new nature. But the promise coursing through these commands is the Spirit's powerful, indwelling presence. So, Paul couples an imperative with an indicative. Believers walk and bear his fruit, but only because the Spirit equips them.[79] God gets glory as he produces his fruits in us and we live them out as embodied beings. Of these fruits, self-control is the only one directly connected to embodied holiness and the call to bodily care.[80]

---

[79] Douglas J. Moo, *Galatians*, Baker Exegetical Commentary on the New Testament (Baker Academic, 2013), 363.

[80] Some believe the fruit of self-control receives little mention in both Testaments, but I disagree with this assessment. Moo, *Galatians*, 366. Many sins discussed in Proverbs result from a lack of self-control. Though the quality may not be explicitly stated, it lies inherent in the sins condemned. Some proverbs demonstrating the lack of self-control include the chattering fool who comes to ruin (10:10), the gossip who betrays a friend (11:13), the lazy person who becomes a slave (12:24), the quick-tempered man who is foolish (14:17), the greedy man who troubles his own household (15:27), the

Self-control is a powerful tool in the fight against all sorts of bodily sins and temptations.[81] To relegate the fruit of self-control to spiritual areas alone reflects the influence of a pious, gnostic approach to Christian living that forgets the call to embody holiness. Still more, it is important to understand that this fruit helps us appropriately enjoy God's good gifts that we can turn into idols, like

---

sluggard who fails to provide for himself (19:24), and the drunkards and gluttons who become poor (23:21). While more examples exist, each of the ones mentioned are the antithesis of wisdom, which is rooted in self-control. Not to mention, in the downfall of Eglon, king of Moab, and Eli, the priest of Israel, the biblical text describes the men by their weight, a typical manifestation of a lack of self-control (see Judg 3:17–22; 1 Sam 4:18). Paul's discussion of self-control to church leaders will be pertinent in chapter 6.

[81] Incidentally, I cannot recall having ever heard a sermon on the fruit of self-control. I imagine most believers have not, which leads me to wonder why this topic is so neglected. One reason could be the church's overall inattention to the person and work of the Holy Spirit, specifically the fruit he enables in believers. Cole seems to agree, saying that the Spirit's fruit is "sadly much neglected in evangelical systematic accounts of the Holy Spirit." Cole, *He Who Gives Life*, 227. Perhaps if Christians lack the expression of self-control, the deeper reason is they remain unaware that they *can* control themselves through the powerful, indwelling Spirit.

food, material things, and even the body itself. Relying on the Spirit helps believers manage all God's blessings in a restrained way.

Because self-control is a specific involvement of the Spirit with the body, it is important to an embodied understanding of holiness. This fruit has definite application for day-to-day Christian living and is especially important to body stewardship. In chapters 4–6 we will revisit the fruit of self-control as we think practically about behaviors that bear on physical health. And given his emphasis on the body, it should come as no surprise that the apostle Paul emphasizes self-control more than any other author of Scripture.

In sum, this chapter detailed Paul's explanation of the triune God's participation with the body in 1 Cor 6:12–20 concerning how the Father, Son, and Holy Spirit are each linked to the embodied experience of humankind. Paul's instruction in a theology of the body through the appropriated works of the Trinity is evident from his mentions of resurrection, redemption, and indwelling. Additional associations between the Father, the Son, and the Spirit, on the one hand, and the body, on the other, include embodied men and women created in the *imago Dei*, Christ's embodied example set for his embodied followers, and the

Spirit's placement to empower embodied living through the fruit of self-control. Recognizing each area of trinitarian involvement with the body, believers value it as God does, submit to his authority over it, and care for it in ways that glorify him.[82]

[82] Greer, "Utilization of a Theology," 146–53.

4

A Historical Argument for the Body

Beloved, I pray that all may go well with you and that you may be in good health, as it goes well with your soul" (3 John 2). Christians appreciate both the differentiation and integration of physical health and spiritual health, tending to the body because they know it succors the soul.

Believers today would do well to follow the example set for us over the centuries: the recognition of an embodied connection that compels the duty to attend to physical well-being. True flourishing cannot happen apart from this understanding, as will be shown in this brief historical analysis, one that is loosely chronological for the sake of my argument.

Early Christian Beliefs

A brief scan of early creeds and confessions reveals a commitment that many believers held to the goodness of bodily existence, in Christ and his followers.

The Apostles' Creed is an early compilation of the apostles' teaching that took shape in the fourth century and was finalized in the eighth.[1] It provides an overview of critical beliefs for the church and, notably, does not shy away from confirming the importance of belief in the resurrection. First, since Christ rose from the dead, Christians proclaim belief in "the resurrection of the body" for those who believe in him. Interestingly, the creed echoes Paul at times in specifying the body as an integral point of Christian belief. Were the body inconsequential to the faith, surely this specific mention would be excluded, especially when a general statement on the resurrection of believers would have sufficed. But early Christians held the importance of the body as a critical belief to be passed down.

Those in the early church not only understood the body's significance, but they were also aware of errant

[1] Gregg R. Allison, *Historical Theology: An Introduction to Christian Doctrine* (Zondervan Academic, 2011), 736.

philosophies that stood against orthodox belief. With the influence of heresies that perverted the person and work of Christ, holding to the fleshly existence of the Son of God was critical to the gospel message. There is no Savior for sinful humanity apart from his two natures, divine and human. Knowing that the Son's assumption of a body confirmed the worth of the human body made in God's image, they maintained the teaching of bodily resurrection. Still more, they were concerned with a present display of faith that did not exclude the body or deny its value.

The Chalcedonian Creed in 451 took up such a defense of Christology, confirming that Jesus Christ is "truly God and truly man, of a reasonable soul and body."[2] Here is that affirmation of a dualistic, yet unified existence of the Son of God, who is both spiritually and physically fitted for human existence. The Athanasian Creed similarly upheld the hypostatic union and is a lengthier statement than Chalcedon on beliefs and denials imperative to the Christian faith. Also maintaining Christ's "rational soul and human flesh," it includes belief in bodily resurrection, that at Christ's coming "all people

---

[2] "Chalcedonian Creed," The Westminster Standard, https://thewestminsterstandard.org/the-chalcedonian-creed/.

will arise bodily."[3] As with other statements of faith, those who composed this creed did not demean the body, neither Christ's bodily existence nor an eternal future characterized by embodiment.

One final compilation of beliefs to consider is the Heidelberg Catechism, a summary of Christian doctrine born out of the Reformation and composed in 1563. A series of questions and answers, the text asks on the Lord's Day One, "What is your only comfort in life and death?" The answer? "That I am not my own, but belong with body and soul, both in life and in death, to my faithful Saviour Jesus Christ."[4] Here we see that the Reformed faith finds comfort in God's authority over the body and its inherent value. If he claims the body, then it is not true that only the soul is the "real you." The body bears significance to present and future life because who you are as an embodied being is the "real you." Furthermore, if the body belongs to the Lord, then

---

[3] "Athanasian Creed," Christian Reformed Church, https://www.crcna.org/welcome/beliefs/creeds/athanasian-creed.

[4] "Lord's Day 1," Heidelberg Catechism, Standing Committee for the Publication of the Book of Praise of the Canadian Reformed Churches, https://www.heidelberg-catechism.com/en/lords-days/1.html.

he must be concerned with how it is treated. Believers will be held accountable for what we do with that which belongs to the Lord. The Catechism affirms Christ's possession of the believer's embodied existence, and our response should be a confident trust that is displayed by a joyful embrace of his ownership. As Christ is faithful, so his followers are called to faithful submission in soul and body to him, seeking to please him in all things spiritual and physical.

As many forebearers of the Christian faith proclaimed the body's significance, believers today must reclaim this outlook, particularly as we live amid a culture that demeans the body. When we recognize that beliefs about and behaviors of the body matter, we will live with distinction from the world, one that sets us apart in our daily conduct. To that end, we turn to a discussion on two of the seven deadly sins.

Seven Deadly Sins

A short historical account of two of the seven deadly sins will show that some in the medieval church recognized that these physical sins would lead to spiritual ineffectiveness, stalling sanctification as an embodied being.

Before Pope Gregory the Great, others had compiled a list of major sins, but Gregory consolidated them into the seven deadly sins that are known today. They include pride, anger, envy, impurity, gluttony, slothfulness, and avarice, with all other sins rooted in these.[5] Though this specific grouping is not found in Scripture, the individual sins are condemned throughout. Of the seven, gluttony and slothfulness mostly find expression through the body. And if gluttony and sloth characterize physical choices, they will undoubtedly impact spiritual matters, as these tendencies never remain isolated to one area of life.

Sloth

Historically, sloth has been understood as laziness, along with an absence of spiritual fervor.[6] While Christians should avoid apathy toward spiritual things as it can have an embodied effect, this discussion will focus on slothfulness as it pertains to the body.

---

[5] Donald William Backus, *The Seven Deadly Sins: Their Meaning and Measurement* (University of Minnesota, 1969), 5.

[6] Solomon Schimmel, *The Seven Deadly Sins: Jewish, Christian, and Classical Reflections on Human Nature* (Free Press, 1992), 87.

Sloth, or *acedia*, was topic in the monastic movement of John Chrysostom, Athanasius of Alexandria, and Basil of Caesarea, who all saw it as a temptation that monks should overcome.[7] Medieval believers reckoned sloth the foremost sin of the seven, as it involved direct offense against God. Sloth meant a life characterized by a resistance toward cultivating godliness. When viewed as complete disregard for effort, sloth is particularly threatening to the Christian who is called to an active faith. Passivity in spiritual or physical matters inevitably slides into sinful activity, which has led some to consider it the chief vice.[8]

Several remedies for a slothful lifestyle were proposed throughout church history. Some include serving others, singing, dancing, praying, or anything that moves the focus off the self.[9] Interestingly, these remedies are not simply spiritual undertakings. They are embodied endeavors, meant to spur on spiritual fervor through physical engagement. Instead of indifference, these purposeful practices turn the believer from a dispirited, apathetic

---

[7] Siegfried Wenzel, *The Sin of Sloth: Acedia in Medieval Thought and Literature* (University of North Carolina Press, 2012), 9–11.

[8] Wenzel, *Sin of Sloth*, 50.

[9] Wenzel, 211–12.

life to the worship of God, who calls his followers to live intentionally for him. Therefore, this calling should inspire believers to develop a mindset that sees physical matters as impacting spiritual matters.

The Sluggard. The book of Proverbs offers helpful awareness against sloth as it presents the qualities of a sluggard, one who is too lazy to care about any of his responsibilities. Reflect on his qualities. He sleeps too much (6:9), likely forsaking his duties (6:9). He disappoints his employers (10:26), ultimately disappointing the Lord. The sluggard is never satisfied, and his path is fraught with hazards (13:4, 15:19). Persisting in apathy, he fails to even care for himself (19:24). He is so careless that he expects to benefit from responsibilities that he never carried out (20:4). His desires are his downfall, and he hates work (21:25). His well-being is ruined by inactivity and negligence (24:30–34). The sluggard is foolish, despite thinking himself wise, and formulates excuses to remain lazy (26:13; 26:16).[10]

Throughout Proverbs, the sluggard is clearly contrasted with one who is wise, upright, and principled,

---

[10] Kenneth T. Aitken, *Proverbs*, The Daily Study Bible Series (Westminster John Knox), 119.

which gets to the heart of the issue. Sloth and lack of discipline in physical matters will impact spiritual matters. The sluggard knows nothing of an embodied holiness pursued through the fruit of self-control.

Gluttony

Gluttony, like sloth, includes both spiritual and physical warnings because the church has historically understood the simultaneous influence of one on the other. Habitual intemperance in anything can threaten soul and body. For the sake of this book, gluttonous behaviors with food and drink are in view here.[11]

Instead of finding satisfaction in God alone, a glutton seeks satisfaction in excess, particularly food and drink.[12]

---

[11] It should be noted that having a weight problem does not always mean one is gluttonous. Additionally, just because someone might look thin does not mean they have a God-honoring relationship with food and drink.

[12] I appreciate Jeff Olson's definition of gluttony as "the immoderate consumption of food arising from the unchecked appetite for something more than, or other than, what the Lord has provided and is therefore judged a sin by God." Jeff Olson, "Once a Deadly Sin: A Contemporary Assessment of the Sin of Gluttony" (ThM thesis, Western Seminary, 2000), 22.

Driven by an appetite that seeks indulgence rather than discipline, believers who struggle with gluttony should reorient their lifestyle choices to ones that prioritize the Spirit's fruit of self-control. Jeremy Taylor, a well-known preacher in the 1600s, understood this need and regularly preached against gluttony. He believed some pleasure in eating was admissible, but going too far in consumption or enjoyment of food was sinful.[13] In many sermons, he severely confronted excessive behaviors exhibited by a gluttonous appetite for food, connecting them to spiritual neglect that could produce ill effects on society.[14] While he often took a forceful tone that would likely be deemed too harsh today, he rightly warned against gluttony as a deadly sin, a caution believers should embrace in the goal of embodying holiness.

Enemies of Christ. Scripture condemns gluttony, often reporting it as a quality common to unbelievers in Deuteronomy, Proverbs, Ezekiel, Philippians, and Titus. Consider the rebellious son in Deut 21:18–21 who is

---

[13] Schimmel, *Seven Deadly Sins*, 145. Scripture speaks of feasting to the glory of God. Celebrating God's goodness in his gift of pleasurable foods is not gluttony when such occasions are in fact occasional and God is prized over the food itself.

[14] Schimmel, *Seven Deadly Sins*, 154.

condemned for his gluttonous and drunken behaviors, activities often associated with dishonoring God. Or King Eglon of the enemy nation, Moab, in the book of Judges. He is described as having a fat belly, the precise location where judge Ehud stabbed him, a belly so large that it concealed the dagger (Judg 3:12–20). The derelict priest Eli is depicted as a heavy man whose evil sons lacked self-control in their gluttonous, dishonorable desire for meat (1 Sam 2:12–17; 4:18). Then come the proverbial warnings that foolish living manifests in gluttony and excess drinking (Prov 23:1–3, 20–21). In Ezekiel, Sodom is condemned for not only being prideful and gluttonous in their lives of ease but also for their fondness of excess that led them to neglect the poor. Driven by gluttonous appetites, they became an abomination before the Lord (Ezek 16:49–50). Jesus was wrongly derided as a glutton and drunkard, qualities that even the misguided Israelites held as ungodly (Matt 11:19; Luke 7:34).

In Phil 3:19, Paul condemns the enemies of Christ as those destined to destruction. Because their god is their belly, they fall prey to their stomachs. Driven by godless appetites, they glory in their shame, a shame evident to God and others as the physical ramifications of gluttony often burden the body. Here Paul clearly indicates that this deadly sin goes beyond eating and drinking too much. Instead of finding satisfaction in God alone, a glutton seeks satisfaction in whatever he can find. The appetite for more, rather than the Spirit's leading, exerts control over the will. The glutton lacks self-control and fails to understand how his choices affect his body. A right understanding of embodied holiness condemns bodily sins like gluttony.[15]

Turning to the Spirit's power within is the most effective way to overcome these undisciplined bodily actions. The fruit of self-control remains the most powerful means against physical sins in the fight for embodied holiness. As this fruit can tame our most out-of-control appetites, it is a potent antidote for sloth, gluttony, and all other forms of embodied sins. Further discussion on self-control, particularly Paul's emphasis on it, is to come.

For now, we turn to a group of believers in the 1600s who viewed the sins of gluttony and sloth through the lens of the sixth commandment, recognizing that these sins can be detrimental to physical health and thwart endeavors of embodied holiness.

---

[15] Greer, "The Utilization of a Theology of Human Embodiment to Address Body Image," 36–37.

Westminster Larger Catechism

In the 1600s, the Westminster divines understood the call to embodied holiness. While they did not label it as such, the point is that they recognized the need for body stewardship. The next chapter will devote more details to this concept, but a reminder of its definition is essential here due to its connection to the Catechism. As Christians, body stewardship requires accepting responsibility for the body by appropriately caring for its needs. So, tending to one's own well-being should be a natural implication of the Christian faith.

The Westminster Larger Catechism argued for bodily care via the sixth commandment, which prohibits murder of another person (Exod 20:13). Their method is instructive for an embodied understanding of holiness as it implies responsibility over the entirety of one's life. The catechism examines the sixth commandment against killing and argues for its extension to include a person's actions against himself and others. Thus, it held the command as encompassing far more than murder. Expanding on the prohibition against killing, the catechism rendered the command in a positive light—that of life preservation, the opposite of taking life. To the authors, the command not to take life was synonymous with protecting, guarding, and preserving life. The Christian's duty was not only working to preserve others' lives but also persevering the very life of oneself.

To the Westminster divines, preserving life meant providing proper care for one's physical existence, or, in other words, body stewardship. They explained that life preservation meant forgoing two of the seven deadly sins, sloth and gluttony, to achieve a lifestyle that does not threaten or damage one's physical well-being. Additionally, their description of what life preservation means is essential to comprehend. They offered both positive and negative aspects in terms of what duties are required and what sins are forbidden to preserve life.[16] In keeping with the purpose of this work, ones that pertain to the body will be highlighted.[17]

---

[16] Westminster Longer Catechism, Questions 135–36 (Presbyterian Church in America Administrative Committee), pp. 274–78.

[17] Commenting on this section of the Catechism, Martin agrees, "I say that the law of God demands that we be concerned about this issue as men of God seeking to live before the face of God with optimum usefulness in the work of God. There must be a concern for our physical and emotional health and vigor." Albert N. Martin, *The Man of God: His Calling and Godly Life*, vol. 1 of *Pastoral Theology* (Trinity Pulpit Press, 2018), 307.

Concerning the duties required, the Westminster divines promote preserving life through sober or reasonable use of meat, drink, physic, sleep, labor, and recreation. So, in efforts for life preservation, the foods we eat; drinks we consume; medicine we take; sleep we get; and habits of work, play, and activity we engage in are all duties that can extend life. When taken seriously, Christians recognize that meeting these basic needs is simply part of living every day unto the Lord and stewarding the body to his glory.

Conversely, the Catechism offers a list of forbidden activities, ones that go against life preservation. It even goes so far as to label these activities sinful. Because bodily activities impact our physical health, they should be seen as avenues that can honor God, but when they fail to preserve our life, they dishonor God. The sins forbidden come in two categories, ones that neglect the means of life preservation and ones that are immoderate. The authors explain that the sins that go against life preservation lead to the withdrawal of life, not only the quality of life but also the actual length of one's life.

To the Westminster divines, neglecting the means of life preservation means failure to engage in the duties required to preserve life—namely, meat, drink, physic, sleep, labor, and recreation. Whether from lack of intentionality or outright apathy, neglecting these duties impacts well-being and vitality. According to the Catechism, failure to preserve our own lives looks like choosing to not eat or drink enough, skipping necessary medication, regularly going without sufficient sleep, preferring laziness over work, and refusing physical activity. Additionally, the Catechism condemns immoderation, like consuming too much meat, drink, labor, or recreation, as sinful. While the intentional decision to withdraw these means of life preservation is ungodly, so are the choices to regularly be a glutton, a drunkard, or an alcoholic or to engage in so much play or exercise that nothing else gets done.[18]

As believers, we should connect these prohibited behaviors to our own lives. Immoderate use of food and drink equates to eating too much and being driven by the idol of food, a gluttonous mindset, and its resultant behavior. Arguably, the types of food and drink one consumes need consideration as well. Frequent consumption of processed foods or ones containing high amounts of sugar, saturated fats, and sodium provide little nutrient content and can be considered contradictory to life preservation.

---

[18] Lainey Greer, *Be Well: Learning to Steward Your Health* (New Growth, 2022), 9.

After all, these foods lead to disease and physical impairment, damage the body, and do very little to steward it. While legalism should be avoided and unhealthy foods are not necessarily biblically prohibited, moderation, reasonable consumption, and self-control are the goals. We would also do well to remember that many of the convenience foods consumed today did not exist when Scripture was recorded. Foods with additives, packaged in plastics, with lengthy ingredient lists may not be the best choice for the health of our body and preservation of life.[19] Still, we can conclusively know that the frequent, habitual intake of unhealthy foods and gluttonous, mindless consumption are immoderate. And according to the Westminster divines, Scripture condemns these practices.

In the end, the Larger Westminster Catechism set the clear tracks toward body stewardship and embodied holiness hundreds of years ago. Yet, for one reason or another, the church has lost its way. Whether from hectic schedules, modern conveniences, or a myopic focus on

---

[19] See the FDA's list of nearly 4,000 chemicals they allow for use in food sold in the United States. Food and Drug Administration, "Substances Added to Foods," last updated September 16, 2024, https://www.hfpappexternal.fda.gov/scripts/fdcc/index.cfm?set=FoodSubstances.

spiritual growth, Christians are in danger of neglecting their bodies and should rediscover the call to life preservation from the Westminster divines. In chapter 5, we will take a thorough dive into the call of body stewardship and the practical realities of preserving life through the means of proper nutrition, sufficient exercise, adequate rest, and stress management.[20]

---

[20] Greer, "Utilization of a Theology," 209–10.

5

Embodied Holiness: Practical Approaches

"So, whether you eat or drink, or whatever you do, do all to the glory of God" (1 Cor 10:31). Christians aim to be wholly holy, submitting their embodied existence and all that entails to the Lord.

Now that we have laid biblical, anthropological, theological, and historical foundations for embodied holiness, the final two chapters shift to a more practical and applicable tone. When believers rightly understand the call to embodied holiness and find motivation from the preceding fundamental layers, we can steward our bodies to the glory of God. To the task of body stewardship we now turn.

Body stewardship involves accepting responsibility for the body by appropriately caring for its needs. Scripture attests to the accountability believers need for their stewardship of time, talents, money, and family, to name a few (see, for example, Deut 15:9–10; Prov 3:9–10; Col 4:5; Eph 5:16). But we should also recognize that the body God fashioned for us is also meant to be stewarded, to be dutifully tended to. God gives us the high calling to manage his creation; we are meant to be responsible caretakers and overseers of his many blessings. Understanding care for ourselves in this light, body stewardship flows from a faithful response to the way God physically created his image-bearers.

As the definition communicates, one aspect of body stewardship is recognizing that God created humans with physical needs, which include the basic areas of proper nutrition, sufficient exercise, adequate rest, and stress management. Per the Westminster Larger Catechism, stewarding the body also requires viewing all physical behaviors as either maintaining life or neglecting the necessary means of life preservation. So, God-honoring body stewardship responds according to the bodily needs God gives us, spurred on by the duty of life preservation by meeting our specific requirements of food, drink, sleep, labor, and recreation.

In following the call to embody holiness, Christians should at least commit to exhibiting a baseline level of care for physical health. While it is crucial to avoid idolizing our physical health, we must also not exist on the other end of the pendulum swing by being apathetic toward our well-being. Maintaining the balance, and equipped with the Holy Spirit's fruit of self-control, we strive toward the goal of body stewardship by relying on the divine ability within us for disciplined living.[1]

Living out holiness in the body and devoting care for it to the glory of God are influenced by the way he designed our body: to require certain nutrients, to improve with exercise, and to experience limitations that require rest and stress management. The next section provides an overview of these four areas, and while the summaries are a helpful resource, they are in no way meant to be a comprehensive guide on these topics.

As the Israelites were commanded to love the Lord holistically as embodied beings—devoted in heart, soul, mind, and strength—these areas of stewardship should

---

[1] Paul David Tripp articulates a clear recognition of the need for body stewardship in the church in *Lead: 12 Gospel Principles for Leadership in the Church* (Crossway, 2020).

foster a mindset of humility. Humility comes with the recognition that you and I are finite beings who require food, activity, rest, and limited stress to not only survive but thrive as embodied beings. This is God's design, but our choices may not always align with it. This misalignment is corrected by heeding the call to embody holiness. To echo the Catechism, when our eating, drinking, lack of resting, and regular stressing go against life preservation, our well-being and ministry ability will wane. As much as these means of life preservation lie within our ability to discipline, body stewardship becomes an integral part of our Christian life that is joyfully devoted to the glory of God.

Designed to Require Nutrients

As the Larger Catechism calls believers to embody holiness by working to preserve their lives, the first means is our need for food. Consuming proper nutrition is an aspect of body stewardship because we understand that God designed our bodies to need various nutrients, which are classified as macro- and micronutrients. Nutrition involves the way nutrients in food break down in the body to provide for numerous functions and maintain physical health. But with the diversity of foods readily available, the confusing reality is that it is possible to eat a lot of food without getting the proper nutrients our body needs. Naturally occurring foods (foods that come from nature) generally contain better nutrients. Processed food items, such as canned foods or baked goods, have been somewhat manipulated but are not as bad as ultra-processed foods.[2] These foods look nothing like their original form and contain scant nutritional value, empty calories, and additives that counteract well-being. On average, Americans consume 60 percent of their total daily calories from ultra-processed food sources.[3] So, as we aim to assess the foods we eat, it is helpful to know the difference between real versus manufactured foods.[4]

---

[2] For more, see Norman Wirzba, *Food and Faith: A Theology of Eating* (Cambridge University Press, 2019); Richard Swenson, *Margin: Restoring Emotional, Physical, Financial, and Time Reserves to Overloaded Lives* (NavPress, 2004).

[3] "Processed Foods and Health," The Nutrition Source, Harvard T. H. Chan School of Public Health, accessed March 18, 2025, https://nutritionsource.hsph.harvard.edu/processed-foods/.

[4] Wirzba recognizes that "the market forces now determining much of the world's production, distribution, and consumption of food degrade, sicken, and destroy life." Wirzba, *Food and Faith*, 5. Christians should be aware of such matters.

Macronutrients

The three macronutrients found in foods are carbohydrates, fats, and proteins. Unsurprisingly, God designed the body to need all three, which means Christians should seek wisdom if considering diets that promote eliminating a whole macronutrient class.

Carbohydrates come in various forms and are generally categorized as sugars, starches, or fiber, and every cell in the body requires them. They break down into glucose molecules during digestion to fuel the body's energy needs. Complex sources of carbohydrates are the best to consume. They take longer to break down and be absorbed by the digestive system, which helps you stay full longer. Complex carbs contain a lower glycemic index, meaning they cause less of a spike in blood sugar. These sources are often browner in color and come from whole grains, brown rice, quinoa, and beans, to name a few. Simple sources of carbohydrates should be consumed less frequently; they absorb quickly in the bloodstream, leading to a higher glycemic index. Examples are usually white in color, like simple sugars in cookies, cakes, and donuts, and often have "enriched grains" on the packaging. Do not be fooled; these highly manipulated grains are not very enriching.

The body does not need any sources of added sugar, so we should limit our sugar intake to twenty-five grams a day. Sadly, the average American ingests nearly three times that daily amount, a regular excess that leads to type 2 diabetes.[5] Fiber is carbohydrate content the body cannot fully break down. Men need thirty-five grams of fiber each day, whereas women need twenty-five grams. Fiber is essential for a healthy gut. But as we consume fewer real foods and more processed foods, fiber consumption is lacking while digestive issues and colon cancer are increasing.[6]

Fats are the next macronutrient found in foods, and the body relies on various forms, known as fatty acids, cholesterol, and triglycerides. They store energy, cushion vital organs, help with vitamin absorption, and regulate

---

[5] "Added Sugar," The Nutrition Source, Harvard T. H. Chan School of Public Health, https://nutritionsource.hsph.harvard.edu/carbohydrates/added-sugar-in-the-diet/. The CDC reported in 2024 that nearly 40 million Americans have type 2 diabetes, though one in five of these are unaware they have it. "1 in 5 Americans Has Diabetes," CDC, https://www.cdc.gov/diabetes/communication-resources/1-in-5-americans-diabetes.html.

[6] Tim Newman, "Why Do We Need Dietary Fiber?," Medical News Today, updated January 11, 2024, https://www.medicalnewstoday.com/articles/146935#benefits.

metabolism along with hormone production. Fats come in a few forms: monounsaturated and polyunsaturated, saturated, and trans fats. Being manufactured, trans fats are the worst form, and the body does not need any for daily functioning. Saturated fats predominantly come from animal sources and should not exceed ten to fifteen grams a day. This means most of our daily fat intake should involve monounsaturated and polyunsaturated sources, as these promote heart health unlike trans and saturated fats. These fats are found in real foods, like nuts, olive or avocado oil, some fish, and seeds.

Proteins are the last macronutrient, and the body relies on their broken-down form, amino acids. They provide the foundation of muscle, bone, hair, and nails, and are essential to many other bodily processes. Eating lean protein sources such as poultry, fish, eggs, beans, and some dairy products is optimal for meeting the body's protein needs.

Micronutrients

Finally, three micronutrients also play a key role in supplying the physical needs God designed. While these micronutrients are essential, they do not contain calories, which reflects their name. Vitamins and minerals, primarily found in fruits and vegetables, assist several body systems and cellular processes. Water is also a necessity, making up 55–75 percent of the body and serving numerous purposes. Despite this overwhelming need, most people walk around dehydrated each day and largely get their liquids from beverages filled with added sugar, cream, and unnatural sugar substitutes.[7] While easy to overlook, if even our drinking matters to the Lord, believers should assess the health benefits of their daily beverages in the call to bodily care.

Meeting the body's basic nutritional needs becomes the goal for believers who desire to steward their bodies to the glory of God. Knowing that he designed us with such nutritional requirements, we should seek to meet them as part of embodied holy living.

Designed to Improve with Exercise

God also designed the body to improve with exercise, as regular exercise benefits every system in the body.

[7] "6 Dehydration Facts That May Surprise You," DripDrop, https://www.dripdrop.com/blog/health-wellness/6-dehydration-facts-may-surprise.

Knowing such benefits gives believers amazing motivation to move their bodies to the glory of God. Cardiovascular work develops the circulatory and respiratory system. The heart pumps blood more efficiently. When in poor health, the heart pumps faster, and a resting heart rate of 80–100 beats or more per minute signals potential heart issues.[8] The harder the heart works overtime, the greater the chance of a heart attack or stroke. However, with sustained cardio, resting heart rate decreases, indicating the heart does not have to work as hard to supply the body. A resting heart rate of 60–80 beats per minute is optimal. Cardiac activity decreases because the stroke volume and cardiac output increase.[9]

Lung capacity also improves with exercise. As your body requires more oxygen to sustain activity, your respiratory system becomes more efficient at taking in oxygen and utilizing it. This enhanced capacity, measured in a VO2 max test, reflects the body's improvement at meeting

---

[8] Resting heart rate can be assessed by lying down for fifteen minutes and then counting the number of times your heart beats in one minute.

[9] Stroke volume refers to the amount of blood pumped out with each heartbeat; cardiac output is the amount of blood pumped out each minute.

its oxygen needs. Getting winded climbing a set of stairs is a good sign that your body struggles to support the increased activity in those moments. But the good news is that with minimal work, lung capacity can improve.

In addition to the heart and lungs, health benefits of cardiovascular training impact the entire body. Red blood cells, temporary endorphins, and metabolism increase. Flexibility improves along with the capacity to accomplish everyday tasks. Amazingly, the risk of chronic diseases drastically lowers, including that of heart disease, stroke, diabetes, high blood pressure, and cholesterol.[10] On top of that, the chances of becoming obese lessen as well as one's stress level. These enhancements are not accidental. Rather, they are specifically intended by the God who designed our bodies to improve with exercise.

Numerous forms of cardiovascular activity are available, many at no cost. Walking is one of the most effective. Just getting a minimum of 8,000 steps a day guards against most chronic diseases that inflict many Americans, and

---

[10] "Why Is Walking the Most Popular Form of Exercise?," American Heart Association, updated January 19, 2024, https://www.heart.org/en/healthy-living/fitness/walking/why-is-walking-the-most-popular-form-of-exercise.

even premature death.[11] Jogging, dancing, playing basketball, jumping rope, and skating are a few examples of other beneficial forms of cardiovascular work that elevate heart rate. The American Heart Association recommends a minimum of 150 minutes a week of moderate activity, a pace at which you could easily maintain a conversation. But this time can be halved to 75 minutes a week of vigorous intensity work, a pace difficult for sustained conversation.[12] Arguably, the most effective form of cardiovascular activity is interval training, which cycles back and forth between moderate and vigorous intensities. Intervals can be done to suit any fitness level. Anything goes, from jogging a lap on the track followed by walking a lap, to pushing hard for fifteen seconds on an elliptical machine and then recovering for forty-five seconds. The point is, you can control

---

[11] "Number of Steps Per Day More Important than Step Intensity," National Institute of Health, March 31, 2020, https://www.nih.gov/news-events/nih-research-matters/number-steps-day-more-important-step-intensity.

[12] "American Heart Association Recommendations for Physical Activity in Adults and Kids," updated January 19, 2024, American Heart Association, https://www.heart.org/en/healthy-living/fitness/fitness-basics/aha-recs-for-physical-activity-in-adults.

your intervals, change them up as necessary, and cut down on the minimum amount of cardio per week.

In addition to cardiovascular work, strength training is recommended; that is, two days of a total-body strengthening routine in which every muscle group is impacted.[13] Weight training strengthens skeletal muscles and bones. As with cardio, the methods and equipment can vary. Whether by dumbbells, kettlebells, and barbells or resistance bands, cable machines, and body weight exercises, when muscles and bones are stressed from an external weight source, they build back stronger. Improvements from weight training include increased bone mass density, lean body mass, and metabolism.[14] Everyday movements become easier, while tendons and joints are strengthened, which guards against injury. Body composition benefits, along with motor skills, coordination, balance, sleep, and self-confidence. At the same time, like cardio, strength training decreases the chances of diabetes, obesity, depression, osteoporosis, anxiety, and muscle imbalances. Such

---

13 "American Heart Association Recommendations."

14 A. Ram Hong and Sang Wan Kim, "Effects of Resistance Exercise on Bone Health," *Endocrinology and Metabolism* 33, no. 4 (2018): 435–44, https://www.ncbi.nlm.nih.gov/pmc/articles/PMC6279907/.

God-given bodily adaptations from exercise should spur Christians on toward an embodied holiness that seeks to steward their bodies through sufficient physical activity.[15]

Designed to Experience Limitations

One practical depiction of the Creator-creature distinction lies in the reality that an infinite God created his image-bearers as finite beings who experience limitations. Two aspects of these limitations pertinent to body stewardship are rest and stress management. Because God purposed physical needs to limit us, we should embrace them by caring for our bodies accordingly.

Rest

Rest is a biblical principle—God set the example, commands it, and promises to restore his creation to an eternal rest. Though the sovereign, omnipotent God needs no rest,

[15] See David Mathis, "Move the Body, Renew the Mind: A Christian Use for Exercise," Desiring God, February 7, 2023, https://www.desiringgod.org/articles/move-the-body-renew-the-mind.

he paused at the end of the creation event to enjoy the fruit of his labor from days one to six. In fact, he blessed the seventh day and declared it holy, showing his limited, embodied beings that right rest is a holy endeavor. He commanded rest in the fourth commandment, declared that the land was to be given rest, and sought to provide rest from his people's enemies in the Promised Land (Josh 22:1–8). Though disobedience left the people waiting for that rest, Christ came announcing that he alone can give rest (Matt 11:28). He also set the example of rest, often meeting alone with the Father for rest. Believers trust that the promise of entering God's rest still stands, and that he will fulfill it when all is rectified in the new heavens and earth (Heb 4:1–11).[16]

Despite these facts, Christians, particularly those with ministry careers, struggle to observe regular periods of rest, a reality I know personally. Whether due to a performance-driven mindset, pride, fear of man, an elevated view of self, or whatever else, it can be difficult to admit the need for and take the time to rest. But understanding God's design

---

[16] See Guy Prentiss Waters, *The Sabbath as Rest: And Hope for the People of God* (Crossway, 2022); Gregory D. Hall, *Rethinking Rest: Why Our Approach to Sabbath Isn't Working* (Deep River Books, 2023).

for us as limited beings helps us humbly acknowledge the necessity. Then, we can practically work toward resting in the Lord while also taking time to rest from work. Rest means intentional inactivity, and because we are psychosomatic beings, rest restores the mind-body connection that stress interrupts. It reinforces trust in God and renews our perspective on the One in control of life's every detail.

Sleep is distinct from rest but is also an essential aspect of human limitation. While God has no need to sleep or slumber (Ps 121:4), his creatures do, making sleep a key part of body stewardship on the way to embodying holiness. On average, the adult body needs seven to nine hours of sleep each night. Regular sleep enhances immunity, decreases stress, and betters our mood and ability to think clearly, while also helping with weight maintenance and decreasing the chance of chronic disease. Regular lack of sleep, however, reverses each of these benefits.[17]

---

[17] Sufficient sleep can be hard to come by, as I unfortunately know all too well. As much as it lies within our control, believers should try to get regular sleep. See the following, which offers tips for better sleep: "8 Secrets to a Better Night's Sleep," Harvard Health Publishing, November 20, 2023, https://www.health.harvard.edu/newsletter_article/8-secrets-to-a-good-nights-sleep.

Stress Management

Managing life's stressors is the last piece of body stewardship, and in our fast-paced culture, it is essential. Everyone battles common sources of stress like juggling work and home life, moving, getting married or having a new baby, starting a new job or losing one, significant illness, the death of a loved one, or financial issues. But for believers involved in ministry work, sources of stress increase, as we will see in the next chapter.

Because stress deals with our inward response to outward circumstances, physically, behaviorally, emotionally, and cognitively, stress impacts us as embodied beings. The reality of our psychosomatic design bears out when we endure stress. We may get physically sick from the fear of a presentation or experience a panic attack upon hearing devastating news. Our physiology is impacted by our psychology and vice versa; this is a good, creative work of the Lord. But when we fail to manage stress, the results can be alarming. Emotionally, stress can make us feel overwhelmed, worthless, depressed, agitated, and unable to relax. Behaviorally, we may change our eating patterns, avoid responsibilities, exhibit nervousness, or use substances to block out the strain of our circumstances.

Cognitively, stress can increase worries, racing thoughts, disorganization, pessimistic tendencies, and rash decisions. While the emotional, behavioral, and cognitive toll from stress is significant, the physical ramifications of stress must not be overlooked.[18]

Amid acute, temporary sources of stress, the body responds in various ways, like an increase in heart rate and slowed digestion. Less serious but notable physical signs of stress include dry mouth, clenching teeth, insomnia, chest pain, headaches and muscle tension, frequent illness or queasy stomach, and hair loss. However, when stress is chronic and from ongoing sources, such as a difficult job or relational situation, the physical response can be life-threatening. Over time, chronic stress is linked to heart disease, stroke, heart attack, high blood pressure, depression, obesity, eating disorders, gastrointestinal problems, and internal inflammation.[19] As the body tries to cope day

---

[18] Elizabeth Moyer, "Six Biblical Methods for Handling Stress," Institute for Faith, Work, and Economics, March 30, 2016, https://tifwe.org/six-biblical-methods-for-handling-stress/.

[19] Mayo Clinic Staff, "Stress Symptoms: Effects on Your Body and Behavior," August 10, 2023, https://www.mayoclinic.org/healthy-lifestyle/stress-management/in-depth/stress-symptoms/art-20050987.

in and day out with continual stress, eventually, it will fail to keep up with the weight of these psychological pressures. When the physical ramifications of chronic stress combine with poor nutrition, insufficient exercise, and neglect of rest, believers should be concerned. But without a biblical consideration of the body, our treatment of it might manifest in these ways. However, with the motivation to pursue an embodied holiness, even in eating, exercising, resting, and managing stress, believers can offer every aspect of their bodily life as living sacrifices in worship to their Creator.

The impetus for this chapter harkens back to the Westminster divines' rendering of the sixth commandment. The command against murder involves more than not taking a life; it is the call to preserve life—the life of oneself and the life of others. The Larger Catechism breaks this preservation into several categories, many of which concern matters of body stewardship, because the writers understood that our bodies are not separate parts of us. We are whole beings whose very existence and personhood relies on the reality of both body and soul. So, in essence, body stewardship is care for self and care for the soul. As embodied beings, tending to aspects of our physical existence is an act of spiritual worship.

From this standpoint, Christians heed the call to body stewardship.

Still, we do not tend to our physical needs, stewarding the body in our own strength. Incorporating these nutritional, exercise, and rest basics requires intent and discipline, efforts that Christians work toward by our unique equipping by the Holy Spirit. Through him, the ability to embody holiness is possible. While inconsistencies are inevitable, Christians can steward the body in ways that support physical health alongside spiritual health.

6

Embodied Holiness: Harsh Realities

But I discipline my body and keep it under control, lest after preaching to others I myself should be disqualified" (1 Cor 9:27). Believers recognize the responsibility of living as constant, embodied examples of Christ before unbelievers.

Given the practical nature of this chapter, we must revisit the initial question in the introduction: Is God honored if his children are spiritually healthy but physically unwell? Referring to factors that are within our control, if God seeks glory even in what we eat and drink, physical matters matter to him. Moreover, the reality of embodiment also suggests spiritual health without physical health will only flourish for so long. Eventually, a neglected physical health will spill over to affect the whole embodied being. But thankfully, the inverse is also true.

After learning the basics of health and wellness, we must consider how they should impact our lives daily, as believers who live as a constant display of Christ, and for ministry leaders whose choices should set a God-honoring example for those under their care. To embody holiness in our day and age may look somewhat different than it did for Paul or Timothy, but the differences do not nullify the responsibility. Understanding our responsibility calls for a sober acknowledgment of how we have or have not previously embodied holiness and cared for matters of physical health. Seeing these stark realities and connecting them with the biblical call to bodily care can provide sufficient motivation toward necessary change.

Embodied Holiness in Ministry

The state of the church's physical well-being directly correlates to the way Christians view their bodies. Acknowledging the need for an embodied holiness falls short when the body is not rightly perceived. If one thinks little of the body, little effort will be given to support it. Where the body is devalued, poor physical health is inevitable.[1] And given our theological argument from Paul to the anti-body Corinthians, this pattern should sound somewhat familiar.

To determine the church's health and discern her related view of the body, some statistics are in order. These cover the overlap between the obesity epidemic and the church, along with the unfortunate occurrence of ministry burnout. The chapter will conclude with biblical evidence that God expects an embodied holiness that accounts for bodily discipline among all believers, but especially church leaders. As I alluded to in the introduction, the church has failed to think rightly about the body, and the evidence for this conclusion is notable. Still, we are not without hope.

Highlighting the following subjects is difficult. These topics can be touchy, personal, and uncomfortable to discuss. In doing so, my aim is not to shame but to prove

---

[1] Bavinck understood this saying, "Temporal life has great value in itself for humanity and also in the goal of life that lies beyond us. Bodily life must be sustained . . . in its well-being and health. This makes moderation in food and drink obligatory. The body is serviceable for work, and work serves health, which can sometimes be strengthened further by exercise." Herman Bavinck, *Reformed Ethics*, vol. 1, *Created, Fallen, and Converted Humanity*, ed. and trans. John Bolt (Baker Academic, 2019), 231.

my paramount claim—that the church needs to recover a biblical view of the body and apply it to daily life. Perhaps part of the predicament we find ourselves in today stems from the reality that these topics seem largely untouchable in the church. But as believers, we need a willingness to confront these issues head-on, combined with a humility that allows for charitable conversation and a necessary clarity that elucidates the problem.

In what follows, a low and even adverse view of the body is evident when confronted with the church's physical health. Currently, the most religious states are also the most obese states, and the rates of ministry burnout in the US have been steadily on the rise for years. These numbers show that, at best, we are so focused on our spiritual ministry that we fail to care for our physical vitality. At worst, we are so convinced that our bodies do not matter that we have jettisoned our health, completely detaching it from our faith.

Obesity Epidemic

Before finding appropriate motivation for physical fitness, Christians must acknowledge that the body is worth treating well. There is a glaring reality that exposes the current Christian conception of holiness and physical health. It is the alarming overlap that exists between religious Americans and the obesity epidemic.[2] The most obese states are also the most religious states. Of the top ten states that report the highest religious activity, eight of them also rank with the highest levels of obesity. The obesity category is based on a body mass index (BMI) of 30 or higher, with morbid or severe obesity beginning at a BMI of 40 or greater. The religiosity list is based on frequency of church attendance and prayer, belief in God, and the individual importance of religion. The top eight most religious and most obese states are Arkansas, West Virginia, Mississippi, Louisiana, Alabama, Oklahoma, Tennessee, and South Carolina.[3]

Now, one could argue that various cultural or familial factors and food insecurity impact the South more than

---

[2] Lainey Greer, *Be Well: Learning to Steward Your Health* (New Growth, 2022), 4.

[3] "Adult Obesity Prevalence Maps," Centers for Disease Control and Prevention, last modified March 31, 2021, https://www.cdc.gov/obesity/data-and-statistics/adult-obesity-prevalence-maps.html?CDC_AAref_Val=https://www.cdc.gov/obesity/data/prevalence-maps.html; "Most Religious States 2024," World Population Review, https://worldpopulationreview.com/state-rankings/most-religious-states. Georgia and North Carolina are the remaining two most religious states with slightly lower obesity rates than the other eight.

anywhere else, which can influence obesity. I grew up a Southern Baptist in East Tennessee, so I understand these factors. Additionally, I acknowledge that poor eating and exercise choices are not always the cause of excess weight or related health problems. However, even in these instances, aspects of body stewardship, or life preservation, are just as essential.

BMI classifications, which doctors frequently use to determine obesity, are not always an accurate reflection of physical health. Muscle mass can increase BMI, and obesity can result from health factors other than poor eating choices and lack of exercise. Still, we cannot observe these statistical realities and throw up our hands as though the numbers do not require self-reflection. Christians should at least admit an inconsistency in applying our faith to all areas of life. These numbers reveal a stark disconnect between our faithful body stewardship—honoring God in our eating and drinking—and doing everything in the body for the glory of God.

A study performed at Purdue in 2006 determined that Baptists have the highest levels of obesity among all religious groups.[4] As the obesity epidemic has only worsened since then, those numbers in the church will have

---

[4] Krista Cline and Kenneth Ferraro, "Does Religion Increase the Prevalence and Incidence of Obesity in Adulthood?," *Journal*

increased since the initial study. Ironically, researchers also found that atheists have the lowest levels of obesity, which is a sad reflection on Christians, who believe in a God of created and resurrected bodies.

Unfortunately, the reality of the church's poor physical health does not end there. The Centers for Disease Control and Prevention (CDC) label childhood obesity a serious problem, with one in five children and teens in the United States classify as obese.[5] Studies also indicate religious teens are at a greater risk of being obese than unchurched teens.[6] Additionally, the U.S. Census Bureau identifies the South, where a strong correlation exists between obesity and disability, as the most disabled region in the country.[7] Importantly, not all disability results from excess weight,

---

for the Scientific Study of Religion 45 (May 18, 2006): 269–81, https://doi.org/10.1111/j.1468-5906.2006.00305.x.

[5] "Commit!," Overweight and Obesity, CDC, last reviewed July 11, 2022, https://www.cdc.gov/obesity/initiatives/commit/index.html.

[6] ABC News, "Faith and Fat: Religious Teens More Likely to Become Obese by Mid-Life," ABC News, March 23, 2011, https://abcnews.go.com/Health/Diet/faith-fat-religious-youths-obese-mid-life/story?id=13204624.

[7] Katrina Crankshaw, "The South Had the Highest Disability Rates Among Regions in 2021," June 26, 2023,

as there are different disabilities with distinct causation. However, the overlap between obesity and disability cannot be overlooked and must be assessed as a potential limitation to the church's effectiveness in the world.

Furthermore, when half of all Americans could be obese by 2030 and nearly 20 percent of kids ages two to nineteen are already obese, consider the future state of the church.[8] Those who become obese at a younger age will experience obesity-related diseases, disabilities, and higher healthcare costs at a younger age. Without significant lifestyle changes, they will die at a younger age, as obesity in childhood can cut life expectancy in half.[9] Inevitably, the

---

https://www.census.gov/library/stories/2023/06/disability-rates-higher-in-rural-areas-than-urban-areas.html.

[8] Melissa Healy, "By 2030, Nearly Half of All U.S. Adults Will Be Obese, Experts Predict," *Los Angeles Times*, December 18, 2019, https://www.latimes.com/science/story/2019-12-18/nearly-half-of-us-adults-will-be-obese-by-2030; CDC, "Childhood Obesity Facts," April 2, 2024, https://www.cdc.gov/obesity/childhood-obesity-facts/childhood-obesity-facts.html#:~:text=Many%20U.S.%20children%20have%20obesity,percentile%20for%20age%20and%20sex.

[9] "Severe Obesity in Childhood Can Halve Life Expectancy," EASO, May 24, 2024, https://easo.org/severe-obesity-in-childhood-can-halve-life-expectancy-global-modelling-study-finds/.

rising numbers of obesity will have a long-term impact on our gospel witness, ministry longevity, church planting, foreign missions, and even more as the prevalence of obesity continues to increase among church leaders.[10]

There may also be an impact on missions. The foremost sending agency of evangelical missionaries, the International Mission Board (IMB), adopted a BMI standard upon realizing that some applicants' physical conditions may become a health liability on the field. Out of necessity, the IMB has included this measurement to evaluate prospective missionaries' physical qualification for service. If those called to the mission field fail to meet the BMI standard of 33 or lower, they cannot report to the mission field until it is rectified.[11]

---

[10] Researchers found that obesity is more prevalent among religious clergy than in US adults. David Eagle et al., "Prevalence of Obesity in Religious Clergy in the United States: A Systematic Review and Meta-Analysis," *Obesity Reviews* 25, no. 7 (2024): e13741, https://doi.org/10.1111/obr.13741.

[11] "Team Member Qualifications and Preclusions," International Missionary Board, https://www.imb.org/go/team-member-qualifications-preclusions/. I have personally witnessed missionaries who are so passionate about the gospel and ready to go overseas that they go on a crash diet just to meet the IMB's BMI requirements. Unfortunately, once overseas, the weight comes

While difficult and uncomfortable to discuss, these realities are better helped when believers engage in honest conversations on such topics.

Ministry Burnout

The last issue at hand is the reality of burnout among those in Christian ministry, and it comes with personal experience. After ten years of working in the local church, I was exhausted in every way. Helping to run various ministries, leading multiple small groups, executing regular events, counseling in difficult situations, and caring for church members inside and outside the church had taken a toll. On top of breaking out in stress hives and developing acid reflux, regular tension headaches, and insomnia, I was also

---

back, and it is a worse type of weight. Crash diets result in weight loss largely from water and muscle, and when the extreme behaviors that can only be temporarily maintained come to an end, weight from fat mass, not muscle, is regained. Once on the field, these missionaries were in worse physical health because instead of addressing the underlying poor habits that led to excess weight, they chose unsustainable methods to achieve weight loss. Mission organizations would better serve their missionaries and donors by equipping those they send with a biblical view of the body that results in basic care for physical well-being.

diagnosed with high blood pressure by my mid-twenties, despite healthy eating and regular exercise. After a few years of medication, I left my ministry job to pursue a PhD. Three months post-ministry work, I no longer needed the high blood pressure medication. It turned out that my stress-related health issues were largely environmental.

While burnout certainly occurs among secular vocations, those in ministry juggle not only the stressors of a normal job but also the additional burden of spiritual work. Paul testified to physical struggles but also shared the daily pressures and anxiety he faced over the churches he shepherded (2 Cor 11:28). Such pressures can feel ongoing in church and parachurch vocations. And if ministry workers hold a low- or anti-body view, they may not take the time to care for their physical health. Combine that with the physical damage that ongoing stress can cause, and the outcome may be a condition that threatens well-being and ministry ability. To avoid burnout, it is imperative that Christian leaders care for themselves physically as they care for others spiritually.[12]

---

[12] Albert Martin places great emphasis on the need for ministers to care for their bodies. He advocates that ministers "seek to attain and maintain an accurate understanding of your present

Ministry burnout arises when our physical and spiritual well-being are finally so overwhelmed that we are unable to snap out of it and do the next thing. A variety of physical signs point to burnout. Fatigue, high blood pressure, insomnia, feelings of inadequacy and cynicism, headaches, numbness, emotional volatility, lack of motivation, recurrent sickness, and gastrointestinal issues are all signs of an overwhelmed embodied being.

Burnout also reveals itself in the occurrence of depression among ministry leaders, specifically pastors. A few years ago, Lifeway found that one in five pastors struggled with some form of mental illness.[13] Still, it is seldom addressed from the pulpit, though over 17 million US adults and a

---

physical and emotional constitution, and engage in a regular but flexible discipline aimed at keeping these two aspects of your redeemed humanity in optimum health and vigor." Albert N. Martin, *The Man of God: His Calling and Godly Life*, vol. 1 of *Pastoral Theology* (Trinity Pulpit Press, 2018), 303. He goes on to say, "I say that the biblical doctrine of man demands that we consider the place of the physical and emotional health of the man of God in the ministry. This principle of the interplay between the body and the soul is even more serious for the man who has been called and equipped for the work of the ministry" (306).

[13] LifeWay Research, "Study of Acute Mental Illness and Christian Faith: Research Report," Lifeway, September 2014, https://research.lifeway.com/wp-content/uploads/2014/09

growing number of children battle depression.[14] Rates of anxiety and depression post-COVID have continued to rise, this alongside the reality that nearly 40 percent of pastors admitted they felt like quitting in 2021.[15] These observances lead to several conclusions. First, the church is ill-equipped to help her people who struggle with anxiety and depression. Second, pastors and other ministry leaders are just as susceptible to these same struggles, if not more. Left untreated, depression can lead to suicide, which the church—even its leadership—is not immune to.[16]

/Acute-Mental-Illness-and-Christian-Faith-Research-Report-1.pdf.

[14] "Major Depression," National Institute of Mental Health, last updated July 2023, https://www.nimh.nih.gov/health/statistics/major-depression; "Data and Statistics on Children's Mental Health," Center for Disease Control, August 19, 2024, https://www.cdc.gov/children-mental-health/data-research/?CDC_AAref_Val=https://www.cdc.gov/childrensmentalhealth/data.html.

[15] Ida Kupcova et al., "Effects of the COVID-19 Pandemic on Mental Health, Anxiety, and Depression," *BMC Psychology* 11, no. 1 (2023): 108, http://doi.org/10.1186/s40359-023-01130-5.

[16] Kristen Kansiewicz and Miles Mullin, "The Truth About Pastors and Mental Health Challenges," Ethics and Religious Liberty Commission, October 25, 2023, https://erlc.com/resource/the-truth-about-pastors-and-mental-health-challenges/.

Depression impacts us as embodied beings. Commonly associated with mental and emotional distress, those who battle it often suffer a variety of physical maladies.[17] Given this overlap, the psychosomatic connection is clear. When turmoil exists in the mind, it is borne out in the body. While God designed the mind-body interaction to promote flourishing, when one aspect suffers, that suffering spreads. Those with depression have a 64 percent higher likelihood of developing heart disease.[18] It is the same with other chronic diseases. One-third of those with type 2 diabetes are depressed; around 25 percent of people who have cancer or stroke history also have depression, along with up to 50 percent of those with an eating disorder or Parkinson's disease.[19] Sadly, the

---

[17] "Depression Statistics: Who Is Affected by Depression?," Depression and Bipolar Support Alliance, https://www.dbsalliance.org/education/depression/statistics/.

[18] "Heart Disease and Depression: A Two-Way Relationship," National Institute of Health, April 16, 2017, https://www.nhlbi.nih.gov/news/2017/heart-disease-and-depression-two-way-relationship.

[19] Richard I. G. Holt et al., "Diabetes and Depression," *Current Diabetes Reports* 14, no. 6 (2014): 491, http://doi.org/10.1007/s11892-014-0491-3; Sara Ulfvebrand et al., "Psychiatric Comorbidity in Women and Men with Eating

list could go on. Whether the physical condition precedes the mental condition or vice versa, the point remains that one's whole embodied being feels the effects due to the psychosomatic connection.

These bleak statistics demonstrate a disconnect in the church between our faith and our bodies. If God desires that his people glorify him with their physical lives (1 Cor 6:20), these findings show we need a greater recognition that our bodies are valuable and that God has authority over them. When we allow these truths to alter our mind-set and shift our heart's affections, we will progress in holiness and pursue physical fitness, aided by the Spirit's fruit of self-control, to the glory of God. Thankfully, ministry leaders can guard against burnout and its effects by recognizing a theology of the body, embodiment, and body stewardship. By possessing a biblical view of the body, both physical and mental health will be positively impacted even by the basics of bodily care.

Now, we turn to the biblical rationale that promotes an expectation of embodied holiness for all believers, with

---

Disorders Results from a Large Clinical Database," *Psychiatry Research* 230, no. 2 (2015): 294–99, http://doi.org/10.1016/j.psychres.2015.09.008.

particular emphasis for ministry leaders who desire to set godly examples for those they lead.[20]

1 Corinthians 9:24–27

In these verses, Paul reminds believers that we are constant, embodied examples of Christ. We must be vigilant or else the way we run the race of faith may jeopardize our testimony before others. To the anti-body Corinthians, Paul likens the Christian life to a physical race where runners compete for a prize. Athletes who desire to win display

---

[20] Grudem understands these issues and addresses them in his *Christian Ethics*. Two sections in his chapter on health are "Physical Weakness or Illness Reduces the Amount of Time and Energy That We Are Able to Give to Any Ministry" and "It Is Better to Be Healthy Than Not Healthy." Wayne Grudem, *Christian Ethics: An Introduction to Biblical Moral Reasoning* (Crossway, 2018). Furthermore, Grudem recognizes body stewardship, labeling much of what I include in my definition as "common sense health habits, such as getting regular exercise, eating a proper diet, getting enough sleep" (659). He continues, "The fact is that most people, at most stages of life, have the ability to make a significant difference in their own health and physical well-being. By their choices of lifestyle and health habits, they can affect the number of years they are able to live and carry out effective work in God's kingdom" (659–60).

self-control in all things for the goal of a temporary, perishable reward. How much more should Christians, who await an eternal prize, live this way? To obtain this imperishable reward we must utilize the Spirit's fruit of self-control. Not only is the prize guaranteed, but the ability to reach it is divinely supplied. So, believers exercise self-control against false beliefs, harmful thoughts, disordered affections, sexual immorality, sloth, gluttony, self-harm, eating disorders, and all other embodied sins. Living without control in these matters does nothing to win over unbelievers, who see the allowance of sins and doubt the sincerity of our faith.

Paul set an example for the Corinthian believers of buffeting, or disciplining (from the Greek *hupópiazó*), his body. While guesses abound as to what he specifically means, we know he was not advocating asceticism, another anti-body mindset that he resoundingly condemns (Col 2:20–23). In sanctification, management of the body is imperative (Rom 6:12–14). Holiness advances through self-discipline in all areas of life, and as a leader, Paul understood that he was watched by many. So, he removes obstacles of sin by beating his body to render it his slave rather than face enslavement to bodily passions. Given the race's duration and difficultly, Paul advocates a pattern of participation, one in which the body plays an integral role. Practicing holiness mandates control over the body, not only in matters of personal faith but also for our testimony to others. Therefore, as believers, we do not live aimlessly, without a goal. Rather, we wholly pursue the prize, even as it means disciplining the body.

Finally, Paul also teaches an important point for body stewardship. Sometimes, disciplining ourselves physically may mean that we must fight against indulging our desires or force ourselves to do things we may not desire to do but know we should, like getting proper nutrition or sufficient exercise. In these ways, this text provides further clarity on a life of embodied holiness.

Titus

In this epistle, Paul advises that living with self-control will distinguish Christians from the world. Writing to Titus, a young pastor in Crete, Paul instructs him, the elders, and all the believers to live differently than the Cretans around them. His reason? As their own poets attested, the Cretans were known as liars, evil beasts, and lazy gluttons (Titus 1:12). Paul explicitly mentions this context up front as he instructs believers living among self-indulgent unbelievers.

Lifestyles lacking in truth, goodness, temperance, and self-control were not to characterize the believers in Crete (1:8).

This context is precisely why Paul stresses the need for self-control. He commands believers to exercise this fruit of the Spirit throughout his short letter to Titus, five times in three chapters (1:8; 2:2, 5, 6, 12). Paul understood that living without self-control meant enslavement to all kinds of passions and pleasures (3:3). It is a life that lacks discipline in one's thoughts, feelings, words, and actions. To lead the church well and demonstrate a life of godliness, believers needed to live with control to be set apart from the Cretans (1:8).[21]

Based on Paul's elder qualifications in 1 Tim 3:2, he again expects a life of self-control to characterize church leadership in Crete (Titus 1:8). In fact, Paul held it as such a critical topic that when presenting the faith to Felix at Caesarea, he summed up Christianity in three words: righteousness, self-control, and coming judgment (Acts 24:25). So, Paul sought to cultivate an embodied holiness among the Cretan believers, wanting them to be distinct. Given his emphasis on self-control amid the lazy,

---

[21] Philip H. Towner, *The Letter to Titus*, New International Commentary on the New Testament (Eerdmans, 2006), 688.

gluttonous Cretans, it is clear followers of Christ are not to live apathetic to physical matters. As laziness and gluttony are fruits of unrestrained living, the juxtaposition here is critical. Uncommon among the unbelievers, the elders and all Christ followers were to display a physical lifestyle that differentiated them from the brutish Cretans.

The connection to body stewardship is clear. Given the statistics from earlier in this chapter, Christians are confronted with the reality that the unbelieving world is largely healthier than many in the church. The world perceives the way we treat our bodies and makes assumptions about the faith based on our body stewardship or lack thereof. As believers, we must learn from Paul, who held the display of self-control, bodily discipline, and stewardship as essential for those who represent Christianity through an embodied holiness.[22]

---

[22] Greer, "The Utilization of a Theology of Human Embodiment to Address Body Image," 38–39, https://repository.sbts.edu/bitstream/handle/10392/6643/Greersbts_0207D10687.pdf?sequence=1&isAllowed=y.

Conclusion

The Way Forward

God commands his people to be perfect, or, completely holy, because he is perfect and completely holy (Matt 5:48; 1 Pet 1:15). Though this expectation will not be realized this side of eternity, believers still embrace the call, fighting for its application in body and soul. And while physical health ought not to be prioritized over spiritual health, the argument has been made that Christians should strive for an embodied holiness, one extending to the body and its physical well-being. Though being healthy does not look the same for everyone or mean attaining identical physical measurements, certain generalities can be made for Christians who desire to grow in embodying holiness.

What Is Healthy?

In some ways, being healthy is a vaunted cultural value. Americans alone spent over $450 billion dollars on health and wellness products in 2022, with a projected growth of 5 percent per year.[1] Paradoxically, despite our spending, we are the least healthy we have ever been, as rates of obesity and chronic disease increase year after year. Being healthy has never been so profitable, and yet, apparently, so unattainable. However, Christians can approach health differently. Our pursuit of physical health should reflect an embodied accountability to our Creator while we await an eternal, embodied state, which will be free from the idealized body standards of this world.

Christians must understand that health is not a one-size-fits-all measurement or goal. It is not about a specific number on the scale or fitting into a certain size of pants. Individuals have different genetics, physical

---

[1] "Still Feeling Good: The US Wellness Market Continues to Boom," McKinsey and Company, September 19, 2022, https://www.mckinsey.com/industries/consumer-packaged-goods/our-insights/still-feeling-good-the-us-wellness-market-continues-to-boom.

makeups, available time, financial resources, and abilities, and are in a variety of life stages. So, to hearken back to the Westminster Larger Catechism, healthy should at least mean that we work to preserve our lives. Being healthy includes looking at general markers of well-being and taking more into account than counting calories or working out six days a week. The following factors should be considered when assessing whether you are in good physical health.

Your General Biographical Information

Knowing your family history is a good starting place for determining your level of health. If there is a history of heart disease, diabetes, cancer, or other chronic diseases in your immediate family, you have a higher likelihood of developing those same chronic diseases.

Your Current Physical Condition

If you already have a chronic disease or your bloodwork shows that you are in danger of developing one, it is essential to alter whatever lifestyle factors have led to this point. If your BMI classification is overweight or obese, it is vital to start tackling excess weight, not only because it can threaten your health but also because it will eventually make daily tasks more challenging.

There is also a classification of "skinny fat," sometimes referred to as thin fat obesity or normal weight obesity. This condition involves having a disproportionate ratio of muscle to fat mass.[2] Someone who is skinny fat externally looks thin but internally has too much visceral fat surrounding vital organs, possessing more fat mass than normal for his or her height, weight, and muscle mass. Typically seen in men more than women, skinny fat is quite dangerous, as the sufferer does not look overweight or obese and may be unaware of internal health. Like general obesity, which is diagnosed at a BMI of 30 and higher, normal weight obesity is also linked to the development of chronic diseases.[3]

---

[2] See Nitin Kapoor, "Thin Fat Obesity: The Tropical Phenotype of Obesity," in K. R. Feingold et al., eds., *Endotext* (MDText.com, 2000–), https://www.ncbi.nlm.nih.gov/books/NBK568563/.

[3] Nicole Golden, "Normal Weight Obesity: How to Manage a 'Skinny Fat' Body Composition," National Association of Sports Medicine, https://blog.nasm.org/skinny-fat.

Work-Life Balance

There should be balance between your work life and your private life. If either one is a continual source of stress, it can certainly impact the other. When a lack of balance and boundary exists, your health can be affected along with important relationships, which also increases stress. Maybe your schedule is so full that you regularly cut back on the sleep you need to get everything checked off your to-do list. Perhaps you have neglected family relationships to spend more time working, which led to marital strain that created an ulcer or anxiety attacks. Or maybe you do not allow yourself to slow down until you are physically ill, when your body makes you take a break. Assessing your schedule to intentionally set boundaries is often an important step in guarding your health as an embodied being.

Diet and Exercise

Your eating and exercise habits are typically the most undesirable factors to address when seeking to get healthier. Taking a pill or a shot, or crash dieting may seem easier in the short term, but those methods are rarely successful in the long term. Good choices regarding eating and exercise weigh heavily on physical health, so they are essential when assessing well-being. Eating out too frequently, failing to eat enough, consuming empty calories, or frequently skipping meals will diminish your health. Similarly, sitting too much, overexercising, failing to get at least 8,000 steps a day, and other poor movement habits will inevitably weaken the body over time. A sober evaluation of health will not disregard these factors.

In the end, understanding what it means to be healthy involves assessing your health as an embodied being—how you feel, sleep, and move, along with critical medical data like blood pressure, cholesterol, and blood sugar levels. Such an evaluation is not legalism, but rather an application of godly wisdom as an embodied being.

Do not miss the reality that your physical health directly correlates to the way you view your body. If it is a hindrance or afterthought to you, chances are your physical health will suffer. But when Christians recognize the amazing things that God created the body to do; appreciate its function; value our psychosomatic connection; and care for our overall spiritual, mental, emotional, and physical wellness, being healthy in a way that honors God is possible. And while the process may sound daunting, it transpires one day at a time. As God supplies daily, sufficient grace, his embodied children walk in it from one day to the next. The Spirit's presence is continual, and God promises sufficient grace for each day. Progress, not perfection, is the goal. Though at times this may feel slow and painful, it is achievable with an intentionality to commit yourself wholly to the Lord.

Finally, with this recognition of health, we learn from Paul and correct misconceptions about the body that hinder an understanding of embodied holiness. Accordingly, we value the body and submit to God's authority over it. Believing in a God of created and resurrected bodies, who became embodied to bodily atone for sinners, and who bodily indwells believers to empower them for embodied, holy living, we live set apart. And while not elevating physical matters over spiritual matters, we think about and treat the body in deference to the biblical text, fueled by the desire to do all for the glory of God.

Equipped with biblical, anthropological, theological, and historical conclusions about the body, and tools for its practical care, we press on. As much as it lies within our control, we tend to our basic health and well-being to fuel a life as Christ's ambassadors. Striving to honor God in everything—food, drink, physical exercise, sleep, labor, and recreation—we work to preserve our lives, knowing that neglect or indulgence in these matters threatens our health. We let Scripture motivate us toward bodily care, looking to the ability supplied by the Spirit, knowing that it is through physical existence that we bear a spiritual witness. Created body and soul, corrupted in body and soul, redeemed in body and soul, sanctified in body and soul, and resurrected in body and soul, Christians devote themselves to God in body and soul to fulfill the biblical call of bodily care and display an embodied holiness.

SELF-ASSESSMENT QUESTIONS

Take a few minutes to think through these questions and honestly assess how you might better care for your physical health.

General Health Questions

- Do I have accountability measures in place to regularly assess my health as an embodied being?
- Am I mindful to steward my body to the glory of God?
- Does my lifestyle reflect preservation, or neglect and indulgence?
- Am I on the cusp of a chronic disease?
- If I have a chronic disease, how am I managing it?
- Do I get regular checkups, especially if I am at risk or have a family history of chronic disease?

Exercise Questions

- Am I moving my body on a regular basis?
- On most weeks, do I meet the American Heart Association (AHA) minimum requirement of 150 minutes a week of moderate cardiovascular activity and two days of total body strengthening?
- Do I take time to stretch my muscles?
- Am I spending too much time exercising?
- Has muscle building become an idol?

Nutrition Questions

- Do I turn to food for stress relief or to manage my emotions?
- Are most of my calories from real or processed foods?
- Am I drinking sufficient water or do most of my beverages contain sugar?
- How many fruits and vegetables do I eat?
- Am I obsessed with counting calories, weighing food, or meal planning and prepping?

Rest Questions

- Do I have a weekly period of resting from work and resting in the Lord?
- Do I prioritize seven to nine hours of sleep each night?
- Do I take time to enjoy nature, music, art, or other restful activities?
- Am I cultivating relationships outside of ministry life?

Stress Management Questions

- Are there sources of stress I can minimize?
- Do I notice myself holding my breath, clenching my teeth, furrowing my brow, or tensing another part of my body to deal with stress?
- Does my mind race with anxious thoughts?
- If I can identify sources of long-term stress, what steps can I take to lessen their impact on my health?

Tips for Incorporating Body-Stewardship Basics

- Take one day to list everything you eat and drink. At the end of the day, sort your list into processed foods and unprocessed foods. Then, work to incorporate more real foods while eliminating processed ones.
- Work these stewardship basics into your daily life by incorporating them into your family's routine as well.
- Ask an accountability partner to regularly inquire about your progress on these aspects of body stewardship.
- If you serve in a ministry leadership role, educate your staff on these areas of stewardship and work toward them as a team for added encouragement and accountability.

SELECTED BIBLIOGRAPHY

Allison, Gregg. *The Baker Compact Dictionary of Theological Terms*. Baker, 2016.

Allison, Gregg. *Embodied: Living as Whole People in a Fractured World*. Baker, 2021.

Allison, Gregg. "Toward a Theology of Human Embodiment." *Southern Baptist Journal of Theology* 13, no. 2 (2009): 4–17.

Allison, Gregg R., and Andreas J. Köstenberger. *The Holy Spirit*. Theology for the People of God. B&H Academic, 2020.

Athanasius of Alexandria. *On the Incarnation*. Translated by John Behr. Greek-English ed. St. Vladimir's Seminary Press, 2011.

Augustine of Hippo. *Literal Meaning of Genesis*. Cited in John W. Cooper, *Body, Soul, and Life Everlasting: Biblical Anthropology and the Monism-Dualism Debate* (Eerdmans, 1989).

Augustine of Hippo. *On Faith and the Creed.* Translated by S. D. F. Salmond. In vol. 3 of *The Nicene and Post-Nicene Fathers*, Series 1, edited by Philip Schaff. Christian Literature, 1887.

Augustine of Hippo. *On the Soul and Its Origin*. In vol. 5 of *The Nicene and Post-Nicene Fathers*, Series 1, edited by Philip Schaff, translated by Peter Holmes, Robert Earnest Wallis, and Benjamin B. Warfield. Christian Literature, 1887.

Augustine of Hippo. *Tractates on the Gospel of John*. In vol. 7 of *The Nicene and Post-Nicene Fathers*, Series 1, edited by Philip Schaff, translated by John Gibb and James Innes. Christian Literature, 1888.

Aquinas, Thomas. *Summa Theologica*. Translated by the Fathers of the English Dominican Province. Benziger Bros., 1947.

Backus, Donald William. *The Seven Deadly Sins: Their Meaning and Measurement*. University of Minnesota Press, 1969.

Bahya, *Duties*. Cited in Justin E. H. Smith, ed., *Embodiment: A History* (Oxford University Press, 2017).

Bartholomew, Craig G., and Michael W. Goheen. *The Drama of Scripture: Finding Our Place in the Biblical Story*. Baker Academic, 2024.

Bavinck, Herman. *Reformed Ethics*. Vol. 1, *Created, Fallen, and Converted Humanity*. Translated and edited by John Bolt. Baker Academic, 2019.

Beck, James R., and Bruce A. Demarest. *The Human Person in Theology and Psychology: A Biblical Anthropology for the Twenty-First Century*. Kregel, 2005.

Berkouwer, G. C. *Man: The Image of God*. Eerdmans, 1962.

Brown, Warren S., and Brad D. Strawn. *The Physical Nature of Christian Life: Neuroscience, Psychology, and the Church*. Cambridge University Press, 2012.

Brown, Warren S., Nancey Murphy, and H. Newton Maloney, eds. *Whatever Happened to the Soul? Scientific and Theological Portraits of Human Nature*. Theology and the Sciences. Fortress, 1998.

Bultmann, Rudolf. *Theology of the New Testament*. 2 vols. Charles Scribner's Sons, 1951–1955.

Burk, Denny. "Discerning Corinthian Slogans Through Paul's Use of the Diatribe in 1 Corinthians 6:12–20." *Bulletin for Biblical Research* 18, no. 1 (2008): 99–121.

Campbell, Constantine R. *Paul and Union with Christ: An Exegetical and Theological Study*. Zondervan Academic, 2015.

Claunch, Kyle. "What God Hath Done Together: Defending the Historic Doctrine of the Inseparable Operations of the Trinity." *Journal of the Evangelical Theological Society* 56, no. 4 (2013): 781–800.

Cole, Graham A. *He Who Gives Life: The Doctrine of the Holy Spirit*. Foundations of Evangelical Theology. Crossway, 2007.

Cooper, John W. *Body, Soul, and Life Everlasting: Biblical Anthropology and the Monism-Dualism Debate*. Eerdmans, 1989.

Corcoran, Kevin. *Rethinking Human Nature: A Christian Materialist Alternative to the Soul*. Baker Academic, 2006.

Cortez, Marc. *Embodied Souls, Ensouled Bodies: An Exercise in Christological Anthropology and Its Significance for the Mind/Body Debate*. T&T Clark, 2008.

Cortez, Marc. "Nature, Grace, and the Christological Ground of Humanity." In *The Christian Doctrine of Humanity: Explorations in Constructive Dogmatics*, edited by Oliver D. Crisp and Fred Sanders. Zondervan, 2018.

Cortez, Marc. *ReSourcing Theological Anthropology: A Constructive Account of Humanity in the Light of Christ*. Zondervan Academic, 2018.

Creamer, Deborah Beth. *Disability and Christian Theology Embodied Limits and Constructive Possibilities*. Oxford University Press, 2009.

Cyprian of Carthage. *Treatise 4 (On the Lord's Prayer)*. In vol 5 of *The Ante-Nicene Fathers*, edited by Alexander Roberts, James Donaldson, and A. Cleveland Coxe. Christian Literature, 1886.

Davidson, Ivor J. "Atonement and Incarnation." In *T&T Clark Companion to Atonement*, edited by Adam J. Johnson. T&T Clark, 2017.

Davis, Stephen T. *After We Die: Theology, Philosophy, and the Question of Life after Death*. Baylor University Press, 2015.

Demarest, Bruce. *The Cross and Salvation: The Doctrine of Salvation*. Foundations of Evangelical Theology. Crossway, 2007.

Eagle, David, Anna Holleman, Brianda Barrera Olvera, and Elizabeth Blackwood. "Prevalence of Obesity in Religious Clergy in the United States: A Systematic Review and Meta-Analysis." *Obesity Reviews* 25, no. 7 (2024): e13741. https://doi.org/10.1111/obr.13741.

Elmore, Vernon. *Man as God's Creation: Layman's Library of Christian Doctrine*. Broadman Press, 1986.

Evans, Ernest. Introduction to *Treatise on the Incarnation*, by Tertullian. Edited and translated by Ernest Evans. SPCK, 1956.

Farris, Joshua R. *An Introduction to Theological Anthropology: Humans, Both Creaturely and Divine*. Baker Academic, 2020.

Ferguson, David M., L. John Horwood, and Joseph M. Boden. "Abortion and Mental Health Disorders: Evidence from a 30-year Longitudinal Study." *British Journal of Psychiatry* 193, no. 6 (2008): 444–51. http://doi.org/10.1192/bjp.bp.108.056499.

Frame, John M. *The Doctrine of the Christian Life*. A Theology of Lordship. P&R, 2008.

Frame, John M. *The Doctrine of God*. A Theology of Lordship. P&R, 2002.

Fudge, Edward W. *Hell: A Final Word*. Leafwood, 2012.

Garland, David E. *1 Corinthians*. Baker Exegetical Commentary on the New Testament. Baker Academic, 2003.

Garland, David E. *2 Corinthians: An Exegetical and Theological Exposition of Holy Scripture*. New American Commentary 29. Holman Reference, 1999.

Geisler, Norman L. *The Battle for the Resurrection*. Thomas Nelson, 1989.

Gentry, Peter J. "The Meaning of 'Holy' in the Old Testament." *Bibliotheca Sacra*, 2013.

Gentry, Peter J., and Stephen J. Wellum. *Kingdom Through Covenant: A Biblical-Theological Understanding of the Covenants*. 2nd ed. Crossway, 2018.

Gramlich, John. "Mental Health and the Pandemic: What US Surveys Have Found." Pew Research Center, March 2, 2023. https://www.pewresearch.org/short-reads/2023/03/02/mental-health-and-the-pandemic-what-u-s-surveys-have-found/.

Green, Joel B. *Body, Soul, and Human Life: The Nature of Humanity in the Bible*. Baker Academic, 2008.

Greer, Lainey. *Be Well: Learning to Steward Your Health*. New Growth Press, 2022.

Greer, Lainey. *Struggling with Body Image: Seeing What God Sees*. New Growth Press, 2024.

Greer, Lainey. "The Utilization of a Theology of Human Embodiment to Address Body Image." PhD diss., The Southern Baptist Theological Seminary, 2021. https://repository.sbts.edu/bitstream/handle/10392/6643/Greer_sbts_0207D_10687.pdf?sequence=1&isAllowed=y.

Grenz, Stanley J. *Theology for the Community of God*. Eerdmans, 1994.

Grudem, Wayne. *Christian Ethics: An Introduction to Biblical Moral Reasoning*. Crossway, 2018.

Grudem, Wayne. *Systematic Theology: An Introduction to Biblical Doctrine*. 2nd ed. Zondervan, 2020.

Gundry, Robert H. *Sōma in Biblical Theology: With Emphasis on Pauline Anthropology*. Cambridge University Press, 1976.

Hall, Gregory D. *Rethinking Rest: Why Our Approach to Sabbath Isn't Working*. Deep River Books, 2023.

Harris, Murray J. *From Grave to Glory: Resurrection in the New Testament*. Zondervan, 1990.

Haykin, Michael A. G. "This Anthropological Moment." *Eikon: A Journal for Biblical Anthropology* 1, no. 2 (2019): 6–7.

Hays, Richard B. *First Corinthians*. Interpretation: A Bible Commentary for Teaching and Preaching. Westminster John Knox, 2011.

Hoekema, Anthony A. *Created in God's Image*. 1986. Reprint, Eerdmans, 1994.

Holt, Richard I. G., Mary de Groot, Sherita Hill Golden. "Diabetes and Depression." *Current Diabetes Reports* 14, no. 6 (2014): 491. http://doi.org/10.1007/s11892-014-0491-3.

Hong, A. Ram, and Sang Wan Kim. "Effects of Resistance Exercise on Bone Health." *Endocrinology and Metabolism* 33, no. 4 (2018): 435–44. https://www.ncbi.nlm.nih.gov/pmc/articles/PMC6279907/.

Horton, Michael. *Justification*. New Studies in Dogmatics 2. Zondervan Academic, 2018.

Irenaeus of Lyons. *Against Heresies*. In vol. 1 of *The Ante-Nicene Fathers*, edited by Alexander Roberts, James Donaldson, and S. Cleveland Coxe. Christian Literature, 1885.

John Paul II. *Man and Woman He Created Them: A Theology of the Body*. Translated by Michael Waldstein. Pauline Books & Media, 2006.

Johnson, Eric L. *God and Soul Care: Therapeutic Resources of the Christian Faith*. IVP Academic, 2017.

Johnston, Erin F., David E. Eagle, Amy Corneli, Brian Perry, Rae Jean Proeschold-Bell. "Seminary Students and Physical Health: Beliefs, Behaviors, and Barriers." *Journal of Religion and Health* 61, no. 2 (2022): 1207–25. http://doi.org/10.1007/s10943-021-01480-7.

Johnson, Luke Timothy. *The Revelatory Body: Theology as Inductive Art*. Eerdmans, 2015.

Kapic, Kelly M. *You're Only Human: How Your Limits Reflect God's Design and Why That's Good News*. Brazos Press, 2022.

Kapoor, Nitin. "Thin Fat Obesity: The Tropical Phenotype of Obesity." [Updated March 14, 2021]. In K. R. Feingold, B. Anawalt, N. R. Blackman, et al., eds., *Endotext* (MDText.com, 2000–). https://www.ncbi.nlm.nih.gov/books/NBK568563.

Keener, Craig S. *1–2 Corinthians*. New Cambridge Bible Commentary. Cambridge University Press, 2005.

Kelfer, Russell. *Control: The Book of Proverbs Contains a Blueprint for a Life of Discipline*. Tyndale House.

Kilner, John F. *Dignity and Destiny: Humanity in the Image of God*. Eerdmans, 2015.

Kleinig, John W. *Wonderfully Made: A Protestant Theology of the Body*. Lexham Press, 2021.

Kolk, Bessel van der. *The Body Keeps the Score: Brain, Mind, and Body in the Healing of Trauma*. Penguin House, 2015.

Köstenberger, Andreas J. L. Scott Kellum, and Charles L. Quarles, *The Lion and the Lamb: New Testament Essentials from "The Cradle, the Cross, and the Crown."* B&H, 2012.

Kupcova, Ida, Lubos Danisovic, Marin Klein, and Stefan Harsanyi. "Effects of the COVID-19 Pandemic on

Mental Health, Anxiety, and Depression." *BMC Psychology* 11, no. 1 (2023): 108. http://doi.org/10.1186/s40359-023-01130-5.

Lactantius. *The Divine Institutes*. In vol. 7 of *The Ante-Nicene Fathers*, edited by Alexander Roberts, James Donaldson, and A. Cleveland Coxe. Christian Literature, 1886.

Letham, Robert. *Systematic Theology*. Crossway, 2019.

Letter to Diognetus. In vol. 1 of *The Ante-Nicene Fathers*, edited by Alexander Roberts, James Donaldson, and A. Cleveland Coxe. Christian Literature, 1885.

Macaulay, Ranald, and Jerram Barrs. *Being Human: The Nature of Spiritual Experience*. IVP Academic, 1998.

Madueme, Hans. "From Sin to the Soul." In *The Christian Doctrine of Humanity: Explorations in Constructive Dogmatics*, edited by Oliver D. Crisp and Fred Sanders. Zondervan, 2018.

Martin, Albert N. *The Man of God: His Calling and Godly Life, Pastoral Theology*, vol. 1. Trinity Pulpit Press, 2018.

Martin, Dale B. *The Corinthian Body*. Yale University Press, 1999.

McBride, Hillary L. "Embodiment and Body Image." In *Embodiment and Eating Disorders. Theory, Research, Prevention, and Treatment*, ed. Hillary L. McBride and Janelle L. Kwee. Routledge, 2019.

Moo, Douglas J. *Galatians*. Baker Exegetical Commentary on the New Testament. Baker Academic, 2013.

Morris, Leon L. *1 Corinthians*. Tyndale New Testament Commentaries. Reprint, IVP Academic, 2014.

Mouw, Richard J. "The Relevance of Biblical Eschatology." In *The Christian Doctrine of Humanity: Explorations in Constructive Dogmatics*, edited by Oliver D. Crisp and Fred Sanders. Zondervan, 2018.

Murphy, Nancey. "Human Nature: Historical, Scientific, and Religious Issues." In *Whatever Happened to the Soul? Scientific and Theological Portraits of Human Nature*, edited by Warren S. Brown, Nancey Murphy, and H. Newton Maloney. Theology and the Sciences. Fortress Press, 1998.

Nash, Robert Scott. *1 Corinthians*. Smyth & Helwys Bible Commentary. Smyth & Helwys, 2009.

Nee, Watchman. *The Release of the Spirit*. Bombay: Gospel Literature Service, 1965.

Newberg, Anthony, and Mark Robert Waldman. *How God Changes Your Brain*. Ballantine, 2009.

Olson, Jeff. "Once a Deadly Sin: A Contemporary Assessment of the Sin of Gluttony." ThM thesis, Western Seminary, 2000.

Origen of Alexandria. *Homilies on Leviticus 1–16.* Translated by Gary Wayne Barkley. Fathers of the Church 83. Catholic University of America Press, 1990.

Paul, Pamela. "As Kids, They Thought They Were Trans. They No Longer Do." *New York Times*, February 2, 2024. https://www.nytimes.com/2024/02/02/opinion/transgender-care.html.

Pearcey, Nancy R. *Love Thy Body: Answering Hard Questions About Life and Sexuality*. Baker, 2018.

Pennington, Johnathan, *Jesus the Great Philosopher: Rediscovering the Wisdom Needed for the Good Life*. Brazos Press, 2020.

Plato. *Phaedo*. Translated by Benjamin Jowett. N.p.: n.p., 2020.

Plato. *The Timaeus*. Translated by Donald J. Zeyl. Hackett, 2000.

Pyne, Robert. *Humanity and Sin: The Creation, Fall, and Redemption of Humanity*. Thomas Nelson, 1999.

Quinn, Benjamin T., and Dennis T. Greeson. *The Way of Christ in Culture: A Vision for All of Life*. B&H Academic, 2024.

Rickabaugh, Brandon, and J. P. Moreland. *The Substance of Consciousness: Comprehensive Defense of Contemporary Substance Dualism*. Wiley Blackwell, 2023.

Roberts, Vaughan. *God's Big Picture: Tracing the Storyline of the Bible*. InterVarsity Press, 2003.

Rue, Vincent M., Priscilla K. Coleman, James J. Rue, David C. Reardon, "Induced Abortions and traumatic Stress: A Preliminary Comparison of American and Russian Women." *Medical Science Monitor* 10, no. 10 (2004): SR5–16.

Rutledge, Fleming. *The Crucifixion: Understanding the Death of Jesus Christ*. Eerdmans, 2015.

Schimmel, Solomon. *Seven Deadly Sins: Jewish, Christian, and Classical Reflections on Human Nature*. Free Press, 1992.

Schreiner, Thomas R. *New Testament Theology: Magnifying God in Christ*. Baker Academic, 2008.

Sherlock, Charles. *The Doctrine of Humanity*. Contours of Christian Theology. IVP Academic, 1997.

Sigurdson, Ola. *Heavenly Bodies: Incarnation, the Gaze, and Embodiment in Christian Theology*. Eerdmans, 2016.

Smith, Justin E. H., ed. *Embodiment: A History*. Oxford University Press, 2017.

Stott, John R. W. "The Gospel for the World: Response." *Evangelical Essentials: A Liberal-Evangelical Dialogue*, ed. David L. Edwards. InterVarsity Press, 1988.

Swenson, Richard. *Margin: Restoring Emotional, Physical, Financial, and Time Reserves to Overloaded Lives*. NavPress, 2004.

Talbert, Charles H. *Reading Corinthians: A Literary and Theological Commentary*. Reading the New Testament. Smyth & Helwys, 2003.

Teer, Torey. "'As the Father Has Sent Me, Even So I Am Sending You': The Divine Missions and the Mission of the Church." *Journal of the Evangelical Theological Society* 63, no. 3 (2020): 535–58.

Tennent, Timothy C. *For the Body: Recovering a Theology of Gender, Sexuality, and the Human Body*. Zondervan Reflective, 2020.

Tertullian. *On the Flesh of Christ*. In *The Christological Controversy*, edited and translated by Richard A. Norris Jr. Sources of Early Christian Thought. Philadelphia: Fortress, 1980.

Thiselton, Anthony C. *1 Corinthians: A Shorter Exegetical and Pastoral Commentary*. Eerdmans, 1994.

Thiselton, Anthony C. *The First Epistle to the Corinthians: A Commentary on the Greek Text*. New International Greek Testament Commentary. Eerdmans, 2006.

Towner, Philip H. *The Letter to Titus*. New International Commentary on the New Testament. Eerdmans, 2006.

Treat, Jeremy R. *The Crucified King: Atonement and Kingdom in Biblical and Systematic Theology*. Zondervan, 2014.

Tripp, Paul David. *Lead: 12 Gospel Principles for Leadership in the Church*. Crossway, 2020.

Turner, James T., Jr. *On the Resurrection of the Dead: A New Metaphysics of Afterlife for Christian Thought*. Routledge, 2018.

Ulfvebrand, Sara, Andreas Birgegard, Claes Norring, Louise Högdahl, and Yvonne von Hausswolff-Juhlin. "Psychiatric Comorbidity in Women and Men with Eating Disorders Results from a Large Clinical Database." *Psychiatry Research* 230, no. 2 (2015): 294–99. http://doi.org/10.1016/j.psychres.2015.09.008.

Vagaggini, Cipriano. *The Flesh, Instrument of Salvation: A Theology of the Human Body*. Alba House, 1969.

Verbrugge, Verlyn D. *1 Corinthians*. In *1 & 2 Corinthians*, vol. 11 of *The Expositor's Bible Commentary*, edited by Tremper Longman III and David E. Garland. Rev. ed. Zondervan, 2017.

Vidu, Adonis. *The Same God Who Works All Things: Inseparable Operations in Trinitarian Theology*. Eerdmans, 2021.

Vidu, Adonis. "Trinitarian Inseparable Operations and the Incarnation." *Journal of Analytic Theology* 4, no. 1 (May 2016): 106–24.

Waltke, Bruce K. *Genesis: A Commentary*. Zondervan Academic, 2001.

Waters, Guy Prentiss. *The Sabbath as Rest: And Hope for the People of God*. Crossway, 2022.

Wellum, Stephen J. *Christ Alone: The Uniqueness of Jesus as Savior*. Five Sola Series. Zondervan, 2017.

Wellum, Stephen J. *God the Son Incarnate: The Doctrine of Christ*. Foundations of Evangelical Theology. Crossway, 2016.

Wenzel, Siegfried. *The Sin of Sloth: Acedia in Medieval Thought and Literature*. University of North Carolina Press, 2012.

Williams, Michael D. *Far As the Curse Is Found: The Covenant Story of Redemption*. P&R, 2005.

Wirzba, Norman. *Food and Faith: A Theology of Eating*. Cambridge University Press, 2019.

GENERAL INDEX

H

I

J

K

L

M

SCRIPTURE INDEX

1 Corinthians